14th November 2015

To Sarah

Happy 50th Birthday

Jimmy Pitts

x x x x

TO RUSSIA
...AND BACK

JAMES PITTS

JAMES PITTS

JAMES PITTS

TO RUSSIA...AND BACK

JAMES PITTS

'The only thing that ever really frightened me during the war was the U-boat peril.'

Winston Churchill, Prime Minister 1940-45, 1951-55

'The Allied seamen showed true heroism in their long and perilous sea passages in convoys, being constantly attacked by enemy forces in the appalling weather conditions of the Arctic. The bravery of these men and women who unsparingly fought for the Victory will be always remembered and respected.'

The Russian Embassy (London) website

'A small group of people played a vital role in something as massive as winning the war.'

General Sir David Richards, Chief of the Armed Forces

'This group made an immeasurable contribution to the Allied forces' efforts, facing the enemy in some of the toughest conditions anywhere on the planet.'

Keith Brown, Scottish Veterans Minister

'Against seemingly insurmountable odds, these men risked their lives to help save a part of the world that was starving, struggling to survive in wartime, and desperately in need of help.'

**Capt. Bob Brannon,
U.S. Navy National War College, Washington**

JAMES PITTS

ACKNOWLEDGMENTS

Thank you

To my family: too many to mention, but you know who you are. Your love and support gets me through the days

To the members of the London and Home Counties branch of the Russian Convoy Club for their friendship: Stan, the two Ernies, Jimmy, Howard, David, Tony, Eugene and others

Those who have crossed the bar: Gordon, Frank, Ted, Fred and others

In memory of Henry Seddon

Lost far too young

In tribute to Cdr Eddie Grenfell

A determined campaigner and fighter who did us proud

Never forgetting

The many young men and women of this country who gave their lives during the Second World War, and the millions of people everywhere who perished in this terrible conflict

And finally...

Dianne. If there's a better wife anywhere, I'd like to meet her!

JAMES PITTS

INTRODUCTION

STEVE PITTS

D ad was well into his seventy-first year when, as a family, we became aware of plans to commemorate the fiftieth anniversary of VE (Victory in Europe). It was the spring of 1995.

My two younger brothers and I, each in our thirties, had been aware that Dad had served in the Navy during the Second World War, but he had shown no enthusiasm for discussing his wartime experiences and our knowledge of this aspect of his life was negligible.

The Government announced a public holiday for 8th May, 1995, and proposed a three-day event at Hyde Park, London. What particularly caught our attention was that there was to be a veterans' centre in which ex-servicemen could, possibly, catch up with their former comrades.

Dad said he had no interest in attending the event. We told him that, along with our mother and other family members, we would like to go, and that we would be happy for him to join us. After private deliberation, he agreed. Next, we set about persuading him to go as the veteran he was. Typically, he ignored us. We persisted and, eventually, he climbed into the loft of his modest three-bedroom, end-of-terrace house on the outskirts of west London to retrieve a box of medals that he had kept hidden away since moving into the house in 1960. Prior to that time, he had kept the collection wherever he had found an unremarkable dark spot.

He saw no reason to show these medals outside the family, but we felt that he should wear them on his blazer. An unassuming man by nature, we could not appeal to his ego, so we blustered that there might be a dress code stipulating that veterans should wear them.

My partner (who shortly thereafter became my wife) sewed them onto the holding band that had been tucked away with the medals. Still, he said that he would not wear them. 'I'll keep them in my pocket, just in case,' he said.

'If the others are wearing theirs, make sure you put yours on,' my youngest brother, Chris, told him.

We drove into London and found car-parking spots surprisingly close to Hyde Park. On a gloriously sunny but windy day, we hustled him into one of the several huge white marquees earmarked for the veterans.

A few hours later, heady on beer, wine and whisky and buoyed by his reunion with men with whom he had shared so much but who he had not seen for half a century, he returned to us. At home that evening, for the first time, he sat down and told us his story of his time as a telegraphist air-gunner in the Fleet Air Arm. That is part of the tale which follows.

Dad makes no claims to being a hero, indeed he cringes at the word. 'I was like everybody else, just an ordinary chap doing what ordinary people did in extraordinary circumstances – that's what we all did,' was how he put it. We can make up our own minds about that.

When relating his wartime experiences, Dad rarely used the pronoun 'I', nearly always 'we'. He did not see himself as an individual, more as part of a team striving to see the war through to its eventual conclusion.

To avoid interrupting the flow of his story, I have researched and expanded on several events mentioned by Dad, and which I think are relevant to his story. These are contained in a separate section at the end of Dad's narrative. These are my words, not his, but they may help provide some background and set the scene for some of the incidents that he mentions.

That's enough from me. Over to you, Dad...

JAMES PITTS

CHAPTER ONE

I was born on 28th September, 1924, in a cramped, dank bungalow in Westfields Avenue, Barnes,[1] a small suburb to the south-west of London. If that date rings a bell, it might be because it was on this day that the first around-the-world flight was completed by a pair of American Army planes. It had taken them 175 days.

I was Mum and Dad's second son, although my elder brother, Sidney, had died 18 months before I was born. He was three years of age when he was struck by a cyclist in the street outside his home. He died as a result of his injuries, although I don't know much about that. I can tell you that he wasn't the only son that Mum and Dad were to lose in tragic circumstances.

I was given the name James, the same as Dad, although I have generally been known as Jimmy or Jim.

The bungalow had been in the family for many years before I came into the world. It belonged to my great-grandmother, who lived in it with us, and it had three rooms, no electricity or gas, paraffin lighting and an old boiler for heating water that Mum and Dad did their best to keep fired up, although I think that was a thankless task. The building was only one hundred yards or so from the River Thames, and it was cold and damp.

It was set back from the street and stood next to a stable that housed a team of horses that were used to pull the coal carts around the streets of our neighbourhood. During the summer months they attracted huge swarms of flies, and there was no escape from them. It wasn't very pleasant.

Three years after I was born, Mum gave birth to another boy, her third son. He was also delivered at home, and the midwife came on her bike to our bungalow to assist with the birth. I was told to stay out of the way, but, after the delivery, I was called into Mum's room to be shown the baby, who was given the name Gordon.

'Where has he come from?' I asked.

'The midwife brought him with her on her bike,' Mum told me.

I went outside to investigate her saddle bag, and I was disappointed to see that there were no more babies to be given away.

I started school a few weeks before I turned five years of age, going to Railway Street Infants School, which later became Westfields Avenue Infants School as Barnes went upmarket and the road was renamed. On my first morning, I was playing piggyback with my new classmates when I was dropped to the concrete floor. I cut my knee open and was sent home.

I attended that school for only a couple of months before we moved a few miles away to Hammersmith to share a small house with one of Dad's sisters, Aunt Amy. Mum's health had been poor, and I think Dad decided that we had no choice but to get out of the cold and clammy property into which I had been born.

This was the first of several moves that each time required me to start afresh at a different school. I was a shy child, and I don't think all the chopping and changing did much to help me with my natural insecurity.

I contracted Scarlet fever,[2] which at the time caused quite a few deaths among children. It was highly contagious, and all my bedding was burned. I was taken into hospital and put in an isolation ward.

I had got seemingly through the worst of it, and I was beginning to feel a little better, when a nurse came into my room cradling Gordon in her arms. He was little more than a baby and I was somewhat taken aback to see him.

I asked what he was doing at the hospital without Mum, and I was told that he had fallen down the stairs at Aunt Amy's house. There seemed to be no outward sign of injury, but two days later he died. Apparently, a combination of delayed shock and pneumonia struck him down.

Mum was only twenty-six years of age, and I don't think she ever recovered from losing two young sons in such tragic circumstances.

It wasn't long before we moved again, to a small flat above a shop in East Sheen, a couple of miles from where we had lived in Barnes. We stayed there for a year before we moved back to Barnes, where we rented the rear half of a three-storey house in Merthyr Terrace.

I didn't enjoy the changes of schools, but I did settle when I started at Fanny Road Infants School (you probably won't be surprised to learn that this school also had its name changed).[3]

Money was tight, and my diet was pretty basic. It sounds a cliché, but tea would often be bread and dripping, or perhaps bread and soup. Mum could only afford to buy eggs three at a time, and we didn't often eat meat, certainly none of the better cuts. When we did have a treat such as biscuits, we bought a small weight of broken ones from the local grocer for a penny or tuppence. Dad was a builder, but whether he worked or not was dependent on factors beyond his control. If the weather wasn't kind, he didn't work and he didn't get paid. If someone else in the chain didn't show up for work or didn't do his job properly, Dad couldn't do his job and didn't get paid. There was no sick pay or holiday pay, nor was he paid for public holidays.[4]

The thought of going away on a family holiday, of staying in a hotel or a bed-and-breakfast, was beyond my comprehension. It was the same for nearly all the families in our neighbourhood – people simply didn't have the money.

The closest I got to a holiday with Mum and Dad was when we got on a paddle boat at London Bridge and went along the Thames to Southend and Clacton. The return journey was the following day, so we slept in an open beach shelter.

I also went on a short camping trip with the Cub Scouts, which I had joined because there wasn't much else for a young boy to do. The pack met in a hall close to my home.

Birthdays and Christmases typically passed with the minimum of fuss, but, naturally, I didn't know any better. The first Christmas I can recall receiving a present was when I was six or seven. I was given a small metal train, and I got down on the floor to play with it. The next day, it was gone, never to be seen again.

I was given a stamp album which was full of foreign stamps, and which I found fascinating. A few days later, that disappeared – I discovered later that Dad had sold it. There were similar incidents, but I have to stress how hard times were. Dad was a proud working man, but this was the time of the Great Depression and it was such a difficult era in which to earn the money required to look after a family.

Our home in Merthyr Terrace was in a large three-storey building that belonged to a couple who were quite well-off. They lived in the front half of the property, while we rented the back half from them. Our landlord was a businessman in the City and he would occasionally go to Cornwall and Devon on fishing trips, sometimes returning with a catch of fish that he kindly shared with Mum. His wife was good to me. She had a grand piano in her lounge, and she gave me piano lessons, although I never took to it. Each birthday, she gave me a big tin of sweets which, to a young lad of my circumstances, was an amazing present. I'd scoff the lot and invariably be sick afterwards!

This couple had a large family living in Acton, a few miles away on the other side of the Thames. They spent each Christmas Day with them, and they invited us to join them at a huge family house, far bigger than any property I'd been in. They had tables laid out through several rooms, and more than twenty people sat down for dinner. There was a starter, chicken with roast potatoes and vegetables, a sweet, wine, coffee...it was a new experience.

We went into a room where there was music and dancing, and they each took it in turns to sing a song. They wanted me to sing, but I was so shy that I could barely talk, let along find the bravado to sing anything!

There was no buses or trains, so we walked back towards the river and crossed it at Hammersmith Bridge. The journey took us a couple of hours.

I was happy enough at Fanny Road Infants School, although I had to take some time off because of a recurring problem with my ears. A couple of times, they were so painful that I was taken to hospital to have my ear-drums unpopped.

When I was eight, I woke up in the night with a terrible earache. I screamed so loudly and incessantly, that Mum went to a telephone box to call for an ambulance. I was taken to hospital, where it was quickly decided that I required an operation.

I was laid on the operating table and strapped down. They put a mask over my face to give me gas and air,[5] but I struggled so violently that I worked the straps loose and I fell off the table. They wrestled me back onto it and forced the gas and air on me.

Unfortunately, the operation was not a success and they had to do it again two days later. This time I was very submissive.

CHAPTER TWO

Mum's health had not been good since Gordon's death. She contracted tuberculosis, which we knew as 'TB' or 'Consumption'.[6] This was a disease that was responsible for a large number of deaths, and those who were fortunate enough to survive often took months or years to recover.

She was in hospital for several weeks, perhaps a couple of months. Dad was working wherever he could find work, and I had to learn to get by on my own. Mum was sent away to convalesce in Godalming, Surrey. Dad took me down there by train to visit her, and I realised how much I missed her.

That Christmas, Dad gave me a toy train that was steam operated in the manner of a proper steam train. It had a copper cylinder that you had to fill with water, with a tray underneath into which you placed methylated spirits. The idea was that you set fire to the spirits, and this heated the water to produce steam to move the pistons, which turned the wheels and got the train moving.

I'd never seen anything like it. I put the methylated spirits in the tray and lit it, but, in my keenness to get the train moving, I had forgotten to put water in the cylinder. The soldering joints melted and the train wouldn't move, and I cried my eyes out. Dad tried to repair it, and it worked to a fashion, but it never ran as well as it should have.

Dad was good with his hands, and he built a crystal radio set[7] – he put an antenna wire on the crystal and picked up the BBC and a handful of foreign stations. After valves were invented, he built a wireless. It was primitive and quite large, but it served its purpose. It was battery operated, and it had several batteries joined together to make one hundred and ten volts. He also built a wireless that ran on electricity, although this was a time when there was no national grid.[8] Barnes was a district that had direct current, DC, rather than alternating current, AC, which was more common elsewhere. Appliances that worked in Barnes weren't much good in other places. Once the national grid was introduced, everybody had the same current.[9]

I moved up from the Cubs to the Scouts, and it was decided to make us into Sea Scouts. Our hall was adjacent to the Thames, and we rowed along the river to Kingston and back, occasionally spending the weekend on a schooner moored at Chiswick Eyot. With this group, I went for an overnight stay to the Isle of Wight, which was one way of getting a holiday.

It was around this time that the Spanish Civil War started. This was a particularly vicious war, and a lot of refugees came to London to escape it. Many of them were put up in the streets around where I lived, with large numbers of families being billeted to each house. These people were poorer than we were, and many relied for their existence entirely on charity. I got quite friendly with a few of these children even though they had few words of English and I spoke even less Spanish.

I left Fanny Road at the age of eleven and went to Barnes

Central School in Lonsdale Avenue. I enjoyed my time there, and at thirteen I sat exams from which I achieved the top mark in the school – I got one hundred and twenty points, and the next boy got one hundred and five. I was quite bright at the time. That earned me a scholarship to Kingston Technical School, which had a good reputation and which specialised in providing a thorough education in mechanics. It had a machine shop, and the idea was to turn out people for a career in engineering.

Each year, the three boys with the highest marks in the school's catchment area received a scholarship, and I was fortunate to be one of them. The school was eight miles from my home, and the money from the scholarship paid for my travel, fees, meals, equipment and everything else that was required. Without it, I would have had no chance of attending the school.[10]

I started there in early September 1938. Six weeks later, Mum was taken into hospital again. The TB had returned with a vengeance, and she never came home. She initially went into a hospital in Sheen, but she was transferred to another hospital in Norbiton, on the outskirts of Kingston, which was supposed to be better able to care for patients with TB. She was there for ten months before she passed away in August 1939.

I often popped in to see her on my way home from school, and I saw her suffer so much. They didn't have the drugs to treat her, and I don't think they really knew what to do. I saw her fade away, and at her death there was nothing left of her – she weighed not much more than four stones.

She was thirty-six years of age. She died three years after the death of her grandmother, who had passed away at the age of seventy-two, and a year after the death of her mother. I don't know how old her mother was because I'd never had much to do with her, and Mum never spoke much about her. Something had happened because her mother's surname was Whitby while her grandmother's surname was Ellis, but I was never told what had gone on.

Dad took me to the morgue to say goodbye to Mum. She was laid out, and Dad told me to kiss her on her forehead, saying that this was the custom. Kissing her dead body, feeling the coldness of it, horrified me. Thereafter, I couldn't cope with looking upon a corpse. That was something I had to address during my time in the services, but that was different, that was a part and parcel of the war. It did not compare to being a lad of fourteen years of age being told to kiss his mother's corpse.

Before Mum's death, Dad had bought a plot at a cemetery in Sheen. It was next to another plot that contained my great-grandmother and several other family members. He paid for a three-person plot, his idea being to put Mum there and later him and me.

Two weeks after Mum's death, on 3rd September, 1939, Britain declared war on Germany.

CHAPTER THREE

During the First World War, Dad had answered Lord Kitchener's call to join up.[11] Apparently, he walked into a recruiting office and signed up for the Army. He was sixteen years of age, at a time when the minimum voluntary enlistment age was eighteen, but he put his age up and they accepted it.[12] He was sent away for training, but, when his mother heard about this, she went straight to the camp and took him home.

Dad came from a large family typical of that period, lots of boys and girls. An elder brother, Jack, was kicked in the head by a horse while serving in the Army and had his jaw moved to one side. Another brother, Sid, was a year younger than Dad. He was in the Coldstream Guards and stood guard at Buckingham Palace. He died not long before Mum of whatever illness was going around at the time, leaving behind three young sons and a daughter.

At the start of the Second World War, Dad was in his late thirties and too old to be called up. He was given the job of collecting any metals that could be used for the war effort. He was part of a team of men who drove around the country to gather iron and steel to be melted down and made into weapons or armour. He often went to the south coast to cut down and take away people's garden rails – anybody who had steel railings of any sort had them confiscated. He worked long hours, seven days a week, and often had to stay away from home overnight.

I stayed away from school for the entire autumn term following Mum's death. Sometimes I was home alone, and at other times I stayed with Aunt Amy, who had moved to South Harrow, or with Aunt Lal, who, with her second husband, had bought a house in Westfields Avenue, Barnes, close to the house in which I had been born. Aunt Lal's first marriage had been to a man who lost an arm during the First World War and who later died. They had a son, Ron, who was my cousin and a few years older than me, and we became quite friendly. I knew her second husband as 'Uncle Charlie'.

I was at Aunt Amy's when I marked my fifteenth birthday six weeks after Mum had died. Aunt Amy invited a few girls from her neighbourhood to the house to help me celebrate. They brought me some presents and we had a cake, and I'd never had anything like that before – it was my first birthday party!

I went swimming at the local pool. I dived off a board but collided with somebody in the water. I dislocated a finger, which flopped back to my wrist. I took myself off to hospital but the doctor refused to do anything for me because he said I needed gas and air so they could reset it, and he could only give me that if a parent or guardian signed a form to grant permission. I explained that Mum had died recently and that Dad was away doing his bit for the war effort, but he said there was nothing he could do about that. This was a Friday, so I went home and spent the entire weekend with my finger dangling loosely against my wrist.

Aunt Lal took me back to the hospital on the Monday

morning and signed the forms so that they could operate. She also paid for the X-ray, which cost ten shillings and six pence, a lot of money. They gave me the gas and air and reset the finger, plastering my arm all the way up to the elbow, which was quite a performance.

I returned to school in January 1940, but, because I had missed a whole term, I was put into another class, and I didn't get on with that. A few weeks later, I stopped going to school entirely, and spent most of my time at home alone. I sometimes took the bus to South Harrow to visit Aunt Amy, who was married to a chap, Harold Gispie, who was in the Air Force. He was a bit of a rogue and he later hanged himself.

I had another aunt in Harrow, Aunt Maud. Her daughter, Gwen, my cousin, used to hang around with a group of people who worked at a nearby Sainsbury's and who lived in basic accommodation above the store. They told me about a vacancy that came with accommodation provided, and I applied for the job.

In the early summer of 1940, the Government embarked on a programme to move children out of parts of London that were likely to be vulnerable to German bombs,[13] and children from Barnes were sent to Surrey or Berkshire.

I was at home, alone, when I opened the door to the deputy head master from Barnes Central School. He told me that all the children from his school were to be evacuated, and he said that he wanted me to join them. I had left that school almost two years previously, but he explained that he was aware of my home situation and that he felt it would be best for me to get out of London and into the countryside. We had a pleasant chat and he told me that he was proud of my achievements at his school. I told him that I didn't want to be evacuated anywhere.

I was offered the job at Sainsbury's, and, with little to keep me in Barnes, I accepted it. I went on a short course at the company's training school in Blackfriars, London, and started work at the store in South Harrow. My wage was one pound a week, out of which they took deductions that included twelve shillings for accommodation. I was left with five shillings a week to live on.

I worked in the dairy and meat sections.[14] My first job was knocking up butter, which I did with a couple of wooden paddles. I also had to roll in enormous cheeses, which weighed around a hundredweight, and strip off the outside and cut them into small pieces.

Bacon came in sides. My job was to take out all the bones, rib them, and slice them into thin rashers. By this time, rationing[15] had been introduced and people only got a few ounces each per week.

The hours were long, but that wasn't a problem for me because I didn't have the money to do anything. I had one afternoon off during the week because all shops closed each Wednesday afternoon, and I had the day off on Sunday because shops did not open. Each Saturday, I started at six o'clock in the morning and worked through until nine o' clock in the evening.

I had no holiday entitlement, and when the store was closed for public holidays I didn't get paid. I got a small pay rise on my sixteenth birthday, but that didn't make any difference to how I was working and living.

CHAPTER FOUR

I had no contact with Dad for almost a year, but Aunt Amy and Aunt Maud got on to him about me. They told him it was wrong that a young lad was getting no support from his father, and that I was living a poor existence. I had no decent clothes or shoes because I couldn't afford to buy any. They told him that I needed somebody to take care of me, and they told me to get over and see him.

Dad had moved away from Barnes and was living in Ealing. He had also remarried, to a young Irish girl who had come over from Ballyclough, a small village close to Mallow, County Cork, to work as a barmaid in a pub owned by a distant relative. The pub was close to our former home in Barnes, where Dad went drinking.

Apparently, they had got talking, the romance was swift, and they married at a registry office. Her name was Nell and at the time of the wedding she was nineteen – just a few years older than I was (although at the time I knew nothing about the wedding). Dad was thirty-nine. He took a job as a milkman, so he was at home a bit more.

They started life in a top-floor flat in Popes Lane, Ealing. They were there only a few months when the house next door to them was hit by what was commonly supposed to be a German bomb. It was in the middle of the night and they were in bed. The explosion took out the back of Dad's flat and their bed, along with Dad and Nell in it, was thrown into the back garden. Fortunately, they were largely unscathed, although a small piece of the bath tub did get stuck in Dad's back. He later told me that he did not believe the damage was caused by a bomb from a German plane. Their flat was close to Gunnersbury Park, where there was a multitude of anti-aircraft gun placements. Occasionally, a shell didn't detonate and fell back down to cause quite an explosion. He was convinced that this had happened to them, although it was easier for everyone to blame the Germans.

They were rehoused in a flat in Chestnut Grove, Ealing, which was close to the gates at Gunnersbury Park. A short while later, they were given a council house in a neighbouring street, Cedar Grove, where Dad lived until his death in 1982.

It was after they had moved into this property, a three-bedroom house, that I was sent by my aunts to see Dad. It was strange to see him with someone else, but I couldn't say anything bad about her, she was young and naïve. I probably wasn't too nice to her.

The war had really stepped up, and close to Sainsbury's was a large gasometer that the Germans tried to set on fire by dropping incendiary bombs onto it. I had been drinking in a nearby pub when I walked out to see all these bombs floating to earth around me. I ducked behind a wall and, fortunately, the bombs didn't set off the gas. A few days later, I dived onto my stomach behind another wall when there was a series of explosions close by. I laid there for a long time after the bombs had stopped falling, just in case!

I worked at Sainsbury's for fifteen months. Dad asked me to

move into the house with him and Nell, which I did, but I was unable to settle. They did their best to be good to me, but it didn't feel right. I walked into an Army recruiting centre to volunteer, putting my age on a bit. They asked me for my birth certificate, which I couldn't provide, so they told me to go away and only come back when I could provide proof of my age.

In March 1941, I got a job working for Sperry Gyroscope,[16] a company that made instruments such as speedometers and compasses for planes and ships. It had an enormous site on the Great West Road, Brentford, a road which for many years was renown as 'the Golden Mile' because of the number of factories that stood there. Sperry's employed between six hundred and seven hundred people, and it was just one of many employers in the area. I started as a trainee Capstan operator before becoming a Capstan setter.

The company in the building next to us was Jantzens swimming costumes, but they were evacuated to the West Country. Sperry's took over their building and formed a war department, and I was sent to work in that. We made mechanical analogue computers which calculated the angles for guns to fire at, and bomb sights for aircraft. The computers were quite big, bigger than a typical washing machine, and I was involved in producing the gears for them – everything had to be very precise. It didn't have circuits or anything like that, and it became obsolete as radar and other high-technology systems were developed.

I joined the Home Guard,[17] which was also known as Dad's Army. We didn't have rifles or uniforms but we were given pikes which had a First World War bayonet welded into the end. With the bayonet, they were several feet in length. We had to parade with them – God help any German who came within five feet of us!

We were kitted out with uniforms and guns, and taken to

Hounslow Heath,[18] where we did manoeuvres and slept overnight in Army sheds. That was good fun for a lad of my age – they built trenches across the heath and we got to throw Mills bombs and fire Tommy Guns.

Several days each week after work, on the Great West Road close to our premises at Sperry's, we took part in exercises that were supposed to prepare us should the Germans turn up at any time. We had to practise finding a place to hide, challenging people we suspected of being German infiltrators, searching for downed pilots, and getting people to prove who they said they were.

On one evening each week, we had to take our turn at fire-watch duty on the roof of the building at Sperry's. We worked in the factory during the day, did our Home Guard exercises, and returned to the factory to stay there throughout the night. There were a few of us, and we took it in turns to sit on the roof and look out for enemy planes overhead or spot fires that needed putting out. When we saw anything untoward, we had to give a warning.

We saw quite a lot of action around us in the night sky – planes above our head, anti-aircraft fire, bombs coming down, explosions and fires.[19]

CHAPTER FIVE

The age for enlisting in the armed forces was widened in both directions as the war continued, and, by the time I approached my eighteenth birthday, it was compulsory for all men to register for National Service on the day after they turned eighteen.

If you left it to be called up, you had no say about where you were placed, but if you volunteered you could choose which branch of the services you signed up for. By doing this, you also made sure you weren't in the ten per cent who were sent off to work down the mines, which was something that nobody wanted to do.

My time in the Sea Scouts had given me an affinity for the Navy, something that was shared by at least some of the other boys in the troop. We occasionally spoke about signing up for a life on the seas. That was on my mind as I made my way to the recruiting office in Acton. In the office, there were the different services present, with a few chaps signing up, and I went to the Navy desk and said that I wanted to volunteer. The man replied, 'Sorry - we've got a waiting list'. He said it was eighteen months long, and, with that, I thought my chance had gone.

I had a look around but couldn't make up my mind what to do, so I decided to go away and think it over. As I reached the doorway, the Navy recruiting officer summoned me and asked, 'Are you interested in flying?' I said, 'What, as a pilot?' and he replied, 'No, as a telegraphist air-gunner.'[20] I sat down, thought about it for a minute or two, and the next thing I knew I had signed on to join the Fleet Air Arm, which was the air wing of the Navy. I was told that training for a telegraphist air-gunner took eighteen months.

I went back to work the next day, and one of the chaps asked me how I'd got on. I said to him, 'I couldn't get in the Navy but I volunteered as an air-gunner.' He replied, 'Don't you know that the average life expectancy for an air-gunner is less than seventy-five hours' flying time?!'

I said that was something that I hadn't been aware of, but, not to worry, there was no immediate cause for concern. I told him, 'It will be eighteen months before I get called up and another eighteen months of training. That's three years before I'll see any action, and surely the war will be over by then.'

A week later I got my call-up papers!

The Navy was losing air-gunners in huge numbers and this was expected to continue as the war intensified. It urgently needed to get its replacements into training. I was told that I had to report within two weeks. If I didn't, my enlistment would be cancelled and I'd have to take my chances with conscription.

I took the papers to work, and walked across the factory to show them to a chap I was friendly with. As I passed one of the big cutting machines, a metal bar fell onto my foot and mashed up my toe. I was taken to hospital, where they strapped my foot and kept me in bed under observation for five days – something they frequently did in the days before penicillin.

On the morning that I was due to be discharged, a doctor came to examine my foot. I told him that I was expected to go into the Navy the following week, but he said that I wasn't fit enough to do that. He said that he would give me a certificate to excuse me, but I went home and decided to still go along.

Shortly before I went away, Nell gave birth to a daughter, Maureen. She was my half-sister but I rarely got to see her as a baby.

In January 1943, I was sent to Skegness for four weeks' initial training at HMS Royal Arthur, a naval base which before the war had been a Butlin's holiday camp.[21] The base was home to 3,000 servicemen, two of whom had lived in the same street as me in Barnes and had been in the Sea Scouts with me! We had all volunteered at different times but chosen the same path. Also there was a cousin of mine, a Wren.

We were billeted in small wooden chalets, two to a chalet. The weather was cold, wet and windy, and it was difficult to escape the damp. I was put in with a chap from Manchester, Henry Seddon. Neither of us had had much experience of life, we were quite naïve, but we were of a similar kind and I enjoyed his company – we tried to make light of what was happening to us, and we became good pals.

For the rank of Naval Airman Two, my pay was one pound and six shillings per week.

Because we would be going abroad for some of our training, we were given inoculations against pretty much everything. It wasn't like getting an injection from a nice nurse at your local doctor's surgery – these chaps lined you up and gave it to you! We were given so many injections that our arms really ached.

We had a Chief Petty Officer who had been called out of

retirement for the war. He had a sadistic streak, and he took us straight from receiving some of our injections to another room to practise lashing our hammocks. When you first lashed them, you had to roll them up tightly and tie them as firmly as you could. But our arms were not functioning properly and it was impossible to roll them up in the way he demanded. He shouted and swore at us, and made us undo and redo them any number of time, but the longer this went on the more our arms ached.

He said to us, 'You think I'm mad, but I'm the only sane one here – and I've got the certificate to prove it'. He had been in an asylum for a time, but they let him out with a bit of paper to show that he was sane!

It was several days before we were able to move our arms properly.

My toe was still giving me discomfort, although, as luck would have it, they waited until the end of the four weeks at the camp before giving us our aircrew medical. By coincidence, the day of the medical was also the day on which I could finally remove the plaster from my toe. It was a good job I did, because the medical lasted a full day. They said that they wanted to test our blood pressure, so we had to jump up and down on a chair fifty times and stand still for one minute to see how the blood pressure responded. If they didn't like what they saw, they failed you.

I passed that particular test, but I had my card marked as 'temporarily unfit'. I spoke to a sickbay tiffy, who looked up my results and said that I had failed because I had a polypus in one nostril – this was a growth on the membrane inside the nose. He told me that they definitely wouldn't let me fly with it, and he said that they would probably try to talk me into having an operation – however, if I agreed to that, I certainly wouldn't be allowed to fly and I'd be sent to some other part of the Navy!

I told him that I wanted to fly, and he said that he'd put me through for a second opinion. He said that I would be told to close each of my nostrils in turn with my finger and breathe in and out through the other nostril. He advised me to take a deep breath and then fake the breathing in and out, which is what I did. I passed! Some of the other chaps weren't so lucky, and they were drafted onto a ship.

JAMES PITTS

CHAPTER SIX

A group of us was ordered to HMS St Vincent in Gosport, Hampshire, a Fleet Air Arm training base for officers, pilots, observers and air-gunners, where we did a further three months' basic training. At its conclusion, we were given the draft to go to the United States and Canada. There were seven of us, all around my age, and, like me, none of them had travelled far in their own country, let along ventured abroad. A sense of comradeship quickly developed among us.

We crossed the Atlantic on the Queen Elizabeth, a luxury ship, the biggest ever built, which had been launched a year before the war started. In 1940, it was commandeered by the Navy and used to take servicemen backwards and forwards between Britain and America. It had been modified for its wartime purposes, but there was plenty about it that spoke of a world about which I'd had little idea.

We were billeted four to a cabin, but that was no hardship. The food was unbelievably good – the ship had been supplied in New York, and we ate like lords!

The vessel was fitted with a battery of anti-aircraft guns and, as a trainee air-gunner, I was told to be a part of the gun crew. I got the night shift. The biggest threat to us came from the U-boats that patrolled the Atlantic, but we were fortunate because the Queen Elizabeth was so fast that she could outrun the Germans. To make it even more difficult for the U-boats to find us, we took a zigzag course.

This was my first encounter with Americans, who were generally friendly and good humoured. I was on gun crew duty with a couple of them when one said in a deep Brooklyn accent, 'Look at the "boid" there.' Without thinking, I replied, 'It's not a "boid" it's a "bird",' and he snapped back, 'Well, it looks like a "boid" to me.' I decided to leave it at that but he got the hump and stomped off.

The speed at which the ship travelled through the water was terrific, and we crossed from Southampton to New York in four days. At one point, the captain got on the tannoy to announce that we were travelling at forty-two knots – a record speed for the ship!

After we docked in New York, we were astounded to see how different everything was in comparison to what we had left behind in England – it was quite a culture shock. At home, so many people were poor, even before the war; in the 'Big Apple' everything seemed to be on a much grander scale. The tall buildings dwarfed those I had grown up with in London, and everybody seemed to drive a big car and wear nice clothes.

Back in England, I had worked in Sainsbury's cutting up people's rations of a few slices of bacon, yet here they seemed to want for nothing. There were shops with rows and rows of cakes and fresh fruit, butchers with all sorts of meats on display, ice-cream parlours, hot dog stalls, burger bars...the war seemed to have had no impact on them.

I couldn't believe my eyes the first time I went into a supermarket and saw the massive array of luxury and basic foods on display. As I walked the aisles, I thought of the little corner shops in England and how the war had caused their stock to run down – when the local butcher or greengrocer had something to sell, long queues formed as news spread by word of mouth, and they quickly sold out.

Apart from locally grown apples, most fruit had disappeared completely from the shops in London, but the supermarket and grocers in New York had an ample stock of all kinds of fruit.

We walked around the shops and saw appliances such as washing machines and fridges – they were years ahead of us.

We spent four weeks at an American naval base in Asbury Park[22] in New Jersey, a few miles south of New York.

A large part of our training was learning how to shoot, something that I took to. They gave us all sorts of guns to play around with, including Tommy Guns and Bren Guns, and we did a lot of shooting with shotguns.

Most of the training was devised by the Americans, and they were quite clever about how they went about it. They had the traditional ranges for clay-pigeon shooting, but they also had a range that was clock shaped, at which they demonstrated how we should fire our guns at different angles. There was a good reason for this: shotgun pellets move through the air at a relatively slow speed, so we had to learn where to aim for when firing these guns. As they said, it was no use aiming at the clay-pigeon as it flew through the air because it would be long gone by the time the pellets arrived. We were taught to shoot so that the target flew into the pellets. This was important for us as air-gunners because, should we be required to shoot at German planes, we had to factor in the fact that they were travelling at nearly the same speed as the pellets.

For the next stage of our training, we were sent off to Nova Scotia, on the east coast of Canada and around nine hundred miles from Asbury Park. We were promoted to the rank of Naval Airman One and told that we would be paid in Canadian dollars at the rate of one dollar twenty-five cents a day – the Canadian dollar was worth around four shillings, which meant we were slightly better off than we had been in England. We also got a standard one-shilling per day flying money, which took us above the ranks.

Our band of seven took the train from New York. We were the most naïve of rookies, weighed down with kitbags, a hammock and a suitcase for personal items, and here we were, thousands of miles from home, making our way hundreds of miles up the coast with nobody to watch out for us! We were told to keep a good eye on our kit because should any of it be lost or damaged we'd have to pay for the replacements – only the first issue was free!

The journey took six days, but, again, it was an enjoyable ride because we travelled in a luxurious Pullman car. We each had our own bed, there was a library, the dining car had food and dishes which none of us had seen before, and the scenery was breathtaking. If this was the war, I thought to myself, I haven't got any cause to complain!

Our destination was the British Commonwealth Air Training base close to Yarmouth, Nova Scotia, where the Navy's No.1 Air Gunners School had been based since opening in January 1943 as a joint Canadian-British venture.[23]

As a trainee telegraphist air-gunner, I became part of a three-man team that included the pilot and the observer. The pilot sat at the front of the plane, and the observer behind him. My place was in the rear.

The first plane I got to go up in was a Swordfish,[24] a two-wing biplane with open cockpits. It had a seven hundred and fifty horsepower Pegasus engine, although, as the war progressed, this was increased to one thousand three hundred horsepower. It was a versatile, wonderful plane that was used as a torpedo bomber, a mine-layer, an attack plane and a U-boat spotter, and it had a reputation as being reliable and trustworthy. The Swordfish sat between ten and twelve feet off the ground. It was a bit of job getting into it, because you had to grab hold of the rungs on the side and pull yourself up, taking your equipment with you.

There wasn't enough room in the cockpit to have your parachute on your back, and we had been told to put it under the radio set. As I climbed into my cockpit, I threw my parachute in ahead of me – it tore straight through the canvas and landed on the tarmac beneath the plane! There was no way I could afford to lose that – the Navy charged six hundred dollars for a replacement. I jumped out of the plane and recovered it, although I was later made to pay for the cost of repairing the canvas – it was just a matter of stitching it up, and they charged by the foot.

When I finally sat down, I could just about see over the side.

As I sat awaiting take-off, I was nervous. But once the plane was in the air I lost my fear, and I found the experience exhilarating.

With the other chaps, I had spoken about the death rate among the Fleet Air Arm crews, but, after that first flight, I felt more comfortable. I accepted that if anything was going to happen to me, it was going to happen, and there wasn't too much that I could do about it.

Fear is a funny thing because it can cripple your mind. You need to confront it, to overcome it, and, once you accept your situation, you are able to function without thinking too deeply about the potential consequences.

The Swordfish had a top speed of around one hundred and fifty miles per hour, with a stalling speed of around sixty-five miles per hour. When we flew into a strong headwind, it sometimes felt as though we were almost flying backwards. Because I was so low in my seat, if I wanted to use the gun I had to rest my feet on either side of the plane and lift myself up.

Many of the pilots I encountered were Canadians who had been training in the Swordfish ahead of being sent to Britain. They were seconded to fly us around, but they seemed to see this as boring, in their eyes flying around aimlessly, so they got up to all sort of tricks to make the day more interesting.

CHAPTER SEVEN

I had my first crash on my nineteenth birthday thanks to one of the Canadian pilots. This chap had been boasting to an RCAF sergeant from the Canadian side of the airfield about the manoeuvrability of the Swordfish, which had been nicknamed 'Stringbag' because of the amount of equipment it was able to carry. He invited along this chap, who sat behind the pilot in the seat normally taken by the observer, while I took my place at the rear.

We went up and the pilot put the plane through everything he could, including taking it into a tailspin and pulling out only a few hundred feet from the ground. He decided that he was going to loop-the-loop, which was my first time and quite something. As the plane circled, we had about 4G of force pushing us down into our seats, jamming us in place. It wasn't too uncomfortable.

He levelled out the plane and announced that he was going to do a reverse loop. He told his pal that this was something that was not done so often – with good reason, as I was to find out. This time we had the same 4G of force trying to take us out of the cockpit. Thankfully, I had my g-string attached correctly and it held me in the plane. The pilot seemed to think that all this was good fun, and he continued to show off by doing a few more manoeuvres and spins. When he'd finally had enough and decided that we should return to base, I spotted oil dripping out of the hydraulic pipes on the wing upright and pointed it out to him. He flapped around a bit, and said that we'd lost all the hydraulic oil and that he needed to put the plane down.

He looked around for somewhere to land, and decided on a field that had a row of trees on either side of it. He took the plane down, but, because the ground was marshy, the wheels got stuck on touchdown and the plane flipped over to lay belly side up. My head hit the RT set, smashing my goggles and temporarily blinding me, while I was upside down and dangling a few feet above the ground. I could smell diesel coming out of the wings, and, as my eyes began to clear, I noticed acid from the accumulator dripping down beside me. I thought to myself, 'One little spark and I am going to be burnt alive.' I needed to free myself, but my weight was pressed on my g-string fastenings and I couldn't raise my body to release them.

I called out to the pilot and his pal, but they had both got out of the plane and had run away. I yelled at them to return to help me. They hurried back and lifted me up by my shoulders so that I could release myself. I dropped to the ground and the three of us made a dash for it.

A small group of farmhands stood nearby watching all this with bemused looks on their faces. One of them was brandishing a shotgun and he said what I thought was, 'Look what I've bagged.'

I didn't hold the pilot responsible because it was just one of those things – planes can fail like anything else.

It was the day of my nineteenth birthday, and I needed a drink. I went to the base bar, where I had a few beers with a chap, Paul Thompson, who shared my birthday but who was a year older than me. The beer was served in Canadian quart bottles, which were slightly smaller than British quarts and which cost forty cents each. We drank from the bottles, but after only two or three of these we were full of gas.

We managed to talk our way into getting a bottle of whisky and decided to head for the nearest town, Yarmouth, a fairly small place of around five thousand permanent residents. The people who lived there had been, generally, welcoming to us, and the local girls seemed to have been quite taken by both the typical age of us teenage trainees, as well as our uniforms. Along with several of the chaps, I had become a frequent visitor to the cafés where a few of the girls worked. I struck up a friendship with one of them, Ernestine, and we started to meet on a regular basis.

There was a problem obtaining alcohol in Canada because they had part-prohibition.[25] You could buy beer or liquor only with a licence, and there were very strict limitations on what you could buy. We could have taken our forty-cent bottles of beer with us and probably sold them for a dollar each.

We drank the whisky neat as we walked towards town, and we decided to sit in a field and finish off the bottle. We agreed that we could do with another bottle, but we didn't have much of an idea where to go to get one.

Yarmouth was loosely divided into four sections, one of which was, to put it bluntly, a little seedy. We knew that this quarter had some speakeasy places, and we ventured into one, which seemed to be basically a brothel. Fired up by the spirit in our belly, we approached the bar and bartered for a bottle of whisky, agreeing a price of ten dollars. It certainly wasn't whisky as I knew it, and it was probably hooch – there was a lot of bootlegging going on to get around the strict rules. But we sat there and drank the entire bottle, and after that I cannot remember a thing. I had no idea how we got back to the camp, and, when I spoke to Thompson the next day, he had no idea either. Even more mystifying, Ernestine thereafter refused to have anything to do with me. I had no idea what I had done to upset her, but she wouldn't even acknowledge me when I attempted to speak to her. Our romance was over not too long after it had begun!

I became a Leading Hand, which was nice because I was given a hook for my uniform and a pay increase to two dollars twenty-five cents per day. Any money that we didn't spend could be converted into sterling for when we returned to Britain.

Part of my training was to get up to a good speed with Morse code.[26] We did 'spx' exercises in which we were required to reach a certain number of words per minute. Each day we were given a test, and, if we didn't make ninety-five per cent, we were required to do an additional hour's training each evening for the ensuing week.

A consequence of this punishment was that you missed the last bus into town, which meant that you were basically confined to base. One afternoon, I failed the test and was given the extra hour, but I wanted to get into town to meet Henry and the other chaps. I saw the bus pull up at the front gate and stop, so I legged it through the camp and sneaked out of the back gate, where nobody was on duty. I ran into the road and put my hands up to stop the vehicle.

Unfortunately, there was a group of officers on the bus who saw what I did and reported me. I was put on a charge. At off-caps, I was called out in front of one thousand sailors and had my hook taken away from me. I was told that I would have to wait at least six months to get it back, and that my wages would also be reduced.

There was an Indian reservation that covered much of the area bordering the camp, and, late at night and on my way back from a night out in town, I occasionally heard some sounds coming from it that seemed a little strange.

The scenery was stunning and, when we were given some leave, Henry and I, along with another chap, Charlie Porter, decided to spend a few days at a little summer cottage at the side of a lake adjoining the reservation.

The lake was about a mile across, and we watched the Indians, in their kayaks, travel from one shore to the next. On exiting the water, they lifted the kayaks above their heads and carried them over land to the next lake.

The lake was enclosed by forest, and we had been warned that brown bears roamed free and could be aggressive and confrontational should they be disturbed. I didn't let that worry me and decided to take a walk, but I got lost amongst the tall trees. I wandered around for several hours as I tried to find my way back to the cottage, but I seemed to be doing little more than walking around in circles, getting nowhere. I became hungry, and I began to wonder whether there were any bears around that might look to take a bite out of me.

I decided that the only way I'd ever get out of the forest was to walk in a straight line until I would, hopefully, emerge from the trees. I positioned the sun behind me and, using this as my guide, walked several miles in one direction until I finally made it to grassland. To this day I still say that, when lost, the best option is to keep the sun on your back and travel in a straight line until you find something to give you direction. However, this has not always proved popular with my family. On a large family trip to Malta many years ago, where I was charged with driving a minibus, I got lost on the way back from a day at the beach.I positioned the sun behind me and drove, only coming to a halt when I reached the other side of the island! I was shouted into turning round and returning in the opposite direction.

Back at the cottage, I awoke early one morning and decided to swim across the lake. I was a decent swimmer and was confident that I would make it to the other side, but around halfway across I got cramp in both legs. I stopped swimming and panicked – I really believed that I was done for. I told myself, funny, but I'd come all this way across the sea and this was how I was going to die. What I didn't know was that Henry had come into the lake behind me. He saw me struggling and swam to me, taking hold of me and swimming me back to the bank. He saved my life because it would have been impossible for me to get back through my own efforts – I thought that I was finished.

I spent the rest of my time at the cottage exploring the land around the banks of the lake, stopping for quite some time to watch the large colonies of beavers building their lodges and swimming freely in the cold water. There were many terrapins swimming among them, and they seemed larger than the ones common to England.

I had decided to avoid the café where Ernestine worked as a waitress, so I began visiting another one in the town. I met a nice girl, Della Doucette, and we started dating. We agreed to get engaged, a testament to our desire to 'live for the day' because who knew what could happen the next day?

Della's sister was married to a fisherman, and they lived in a village around twelve miles up the coast from Yarmouth. The village was tiny and I doubt that there was more than ten houses in it.

Della's sister invited me to spend Christmas with them, which was nice, although going into their house for the first time was like entering a different world, not least because their front room was laid out with fishing nets in frames that were being repaired in preparation for the resumption of fishing in the spring.

One of their main crops was lobster,[27] a big industry in this part of a country responsible for what I was told was around half of the world's supply. Regulations specified that lobsters under ten inches in length had to be returned to the sea, but Della's brother-in-law and his fellow fishermen tended to ignore this law when it suited them. They could not sell the undersized lobsters, so they kept them to eat themselves, which they did by frying them in butter. This was the first time that I had tasted such a delicacy, and it gave me a taste for lobster that has remained with me to this day.

Outside in the yard, where the snow was piled high and the temperature was below freezing all winter, the couple kept a side of beef that was frozen solid. When they fancied a beef dish or a steak, they trimmed cuts from it.

Christmas dinner was what they called 'Rappie pie', which was duck and beef in a strong sauce, and, again, tasted wonderful. After dinner, we spent the rest of the day visiting the other houses in the village, at each one being given a drink to celebrate.

I returned to the base to finish my training, which included seven flights in the rear of a Swordfish shooting at a drogue being dragged behind another aircraft. We were instructed to fire two hundred rounds of ammunition at the target, which meant each flight lasted for around forty minutes. After landing, we had to put our empty cartridges into a special container, which took another fifteen minutes or so.

This was mid-winter, and the temperature peaked at around minus ten degrees Fahrenheit (-23oC) and dropped rapidly in the late afternoon. We were given leather masks to protect our faces from the frost, but these were not very effective and the wind stung our cheeks bright red.

The drogue blew about in the wind, moving from side to side, which made it all the harder to target. Each time we went up it seemed colder then the previous flight – something that had been seemingly impossible at the time – and it became increasingly difficult to fix on the target.

The tail of the plane which was pulling the drogue got hit a few times, although the only damage was to make a few holes in the canvas.

By the time we went up for the last time, I was so cold that I didn't manage to fire all the required rounds. I was shivering uncontrollably and my hands were all but locked onto the gun handles. However, I managed to pass the course, although some of the other air-gunners were not so lucky and failed, which meant they had to get up there in the cold and do it all again.

That brought to an end my time in Yarmouth, and seven of us were drafted to an American naval air base in Lewiston, Maine,[28] for four weeks. Again we travelled by train, although I got a surprise when Ernestine and the owner of the café at which she worked turned up at the station to send us on our way with sandwiches and drinks. I didn't see the point in bringing up what I had done to cause her to refuse to speak to me, but I did appreciate the gesture.

I departed still engaged to Della, pledging our love to each other and promising to keep in touch, although our relationship did not survive the subsequent separation and I never saw her again.

The weather in Lewiston was almost as harsh as it had been in Nova Scotia, and it was snowing heavily on our arrival. On our second morning at the base, we awoke to find that more than two feet of snow had fallen during the night – when we attempted to leave our barracks we couldn't get the door open for the weight of all the snow. We had to force the door and dig out a pathway to the mess room, an effort that we were willing to make because otherwise we would have missed out on our mealtimes!

The following morning we woke to find that an even larger quantity of snow had fallen overnight, and again we spent the morning shovelling it out of the way so that we could get to the mess room for breakfast.

We were seconded to an American Lieutenant to take us through further gunnery instruction. He seemed to know what he was doing, and he showed us how to strip down the Browning .50 machine gun and reassemble it. The only problems were that he had a thick Deep South accent and that called the various parts by their American names. We were scratching our heads a bit, so I said to him, 'Hold on a minute – there are seven of us and only one of you, so can I suggest that you learn our English terms, which will make it easier for us to understand what you want us to do.'

That didn't go down too well, and the next day a different officer took charge of the training – I think the previous one had had enough of the bolshie English!

After completing this part of our training, we were transferred to a naval air station in Quincy, a suburb of Boston, Massachusetts,[29] to become part of 856 Squadron (Fleet Air Arm torpedo squadron).[30]

The Swordfish planes that we had flown in Canada were replaced by Grumman Avengers,[31] which had first been used in the United States in 1942. We called them Tarpons, although we eventually took to using the name Avenger as well.

One of the early navigational training exercises saw me go up with a pilot and an observer. It was a four hundred-mile exercise, which meant that we had to fly in a straight line for one hundred miles, turn right and fly another one hundred miles before doing the same again and again to complete a square shape. When we had completed what we thought was our four hundred miles, we wanted to land, but we didn't recognise any of the land beneath us. We had no idea whether we were north or south of Boston and the observer, who was supposed to have worked all this out, didn't seem to have much of a clue. We flew round and round, with the pilot becoming increasingly frustrated.

Eventually, we spotted a small provincial airfield. The pilot put the plane down and we taxied along to where a group of people were standing beside a small collection of light aircraft. They had their mouths open and looked at us as if to say what on earth is this plane with English markings doing at their little airfield? The pilot called a chap over and asked him for directions to Boston. Apparently, we were over one hundred miles away, although at least we were able to ask somebody for help — something we couldn't have done had we been one hundred miles out to sea!

We took off and returned to the base. I met up with Henry, who had been sent to the naval air station a month ahead of me and had been put in a different squadron, the idea behind that being to mix up the squadrons so that six rookie air-gunners were put in with six air-gunners who had seen action. It was the same for pilots and observers.

We had a nice chat and, because we were both on leave the following day, we made arrangements to meet up for a drink.

As part of our training, we had to do a number of hours of night flying, and he told me that he was due up that night. I went back to my barrack. When I went into the mess room for breakfast the following morning, I was informed that Henry had been lost — his plane had gone down in Boston harbour and there was no trace of it or the crew.

I felt such a loss, and after that I found it very difficult to get close to anyone. That feeling stayed with me for many years, long after the war. It wasn't something I dwelt on, but I did become wary about getting too friendly with anyone.

JAMES PITTS

CHAPTER EIGHT

There was a large number of British servicemen at the base in Boston. Many of them were like us, in transit, there for three months before moving on. But there was also a band of men who were stationed there on a semi-permanent basis and had been there for some time. These men had permission to take part-time jobs. Not everybody wanted to do that, but there was a number who did.

To get a job, you required a Green Card. British servicemen had permission to apply for one, and these were typically granted and, in many cases, treasured. However, there were a number of men who, once they had received their card, scarpered. Most of them cleared off to other parts of the States where it might not be so easy to track them down, but one chap stayed in Boston and got a job driving the buses. He was put on the route that served our base, and, each time he approached it, he stuck two fingers up and drove on. He did this to an officer, who got so angry that he reported the matter to the bus company. The driver was investigated and it was discovered that he was a deserter. He was hauled back to the base and put on a charge!

Our three months at the naval air base came to an end, and it was time to return to Britain. I had been away for more than a year.

Our planes were taken to Norfolk, Virginia, to meet up with the carrier that was to take us across the Atlantic. As well as the crew, fifty planes were loaded onto HMS Smiter,[32] a ship that we had taken possession of from America under a lease-lend agreement.[33]

The carrier made its way up the coast and docked at New York. It was due to leave for Britain the next day. I asked around to find somebody to go ashore with, but there were no takers – it seemed nobody wanted to leave the ship. I eventually found a chap who was up for a drink, so we headed into the city to find a bar.

Because we were only nineteen years of age, we had a problem with buying alcohol in the United States, where the drinking age in some states was as high as twenty-one. When you went into a bar, you were required to show your Navy pass, so I doctored mine, changing my year of birth from 1924 to 1920. Back on base, I had to return the date to 1924 because had the deception been spotted I would have been up on another charge. The pass had got a bit messy by the time I was due to sail home, although nobody picked me up on it.

We made our way to Times Square and found a bar. The date was 6th June, 1944.

We got our beers and sat at the window, looking out. We could see the famous electronic news ticker going around, giving a brief summary of the latest events in the war. Around midday, it announced the news about D-Day and the invasion of Normandy.

People stopped to read the news ticker, and some of them saw us sitting in the bar. We were in uniform. A few people came into the bar to buy us a drink, then more followed and did the same. We stayed in that bar until five o'clock the following morning and still had enough money to buy some breakfast before going back to the ship. Many times in the years since, I have been asked what I was doing on D-Day – the honest answer is that I was in a bar in New York getting blinding drunk on other people's money!

We crossed the Atlantic in convoy, as far as I am aware without any great drama other than some brief contact with enemy submarines.

At one end of the carrier, there was a skeet shooting station at which we got to shoot with shotguns at clay discs flung into the air over the sea.

I was quite good at it, and the ship's Commander thought he was pretty good at it as well. He watched me shooting, and said to me, 'You think you're good – I'll take you on.' He offered me a wager – two hundred cigarettes. I said fair enough, and we did our shooting watched by a fair gathering of the crew. I got twenty out of twenty, but he missed with one shot. He gave me the cigarettes, which, because the ship had been stocked in the States, were American – a valuable prize!

We had a cigarette ration, which was a free issue of the Navy's own rolled cigarettes, but if you wanted filtered cigarettes you had to buy them, and they were very expensive.

JAMES PITTS

CHAPTER NINE

Our return to Britain on HMS Smiter saw us arrive off Formby Light, around twenty miles out of Liverpool, on 20th June. The ship was put into Gladstone Dock to be unloaded.

Because the ship had been equipped in the States, it was well fitted and the equipment was of American quality, which was vastly superior to that in Britain.

One of the ship's crew was a man named McGinty, a Leading Seaman who looked just like the man on the Player's Cigarettes packets, with full beard and moustache. He went away and returned to the dock with a lorry. He got up a working party and took a lot of stuff out of the stores to load onto the vehicle, things like blankets, kitchen utensils, towels, tinned food, all sorts of stuff. He drove away and sold the lot in the surrounding streets.

Our planes were unloaded by crane and towed through Liverpool to Speke, from where all twelve were flown to RNAS Machrihanish,[34] on the Mull of Kintyre on the west coast of

Scotland.

We were given a leave of 16 days, so I headed back to London. Nell was again pregnant, but this was not a good time to be in the capital because the Germans had developed a flying bomb, the V-1,[35] which was causing an awful lot of destruction.

There were days when more than one hundred of these bombs, which we called 'doodlebugs' or 'buzz bombs', landed on London, and they were responsible for causing thousands of deaths and plenty of damage to buildings.

I was walking in Gunnersbury Park when I saw a V-1 directly overhead. I hid behind a tree, although that wouldn't have done me much good. The V-1 made quite a noise as it flew through the air, but the scary bit came when it fell silent because that meant that the engine had stopped and it was about to come down. The short silence before it hit was unnerving because you had no idea where it was going to strike – you simply had to wait for the explosion. I hid behind the tree listening to the noise of the ack-ack guns trying to hit the bomb, and wondered what on earth I was doing there.

I wanted to get back to Machrihanish, where I felt safer, although that feeling didn't last long because, on my return to the base, I had my second crash.

Our training commenced with a three-week bombing course that was quite intense, and I had my first taste of mine-laying, an operation that the Avengers specialised in. We were taught how to fly in formation because during operations the planes flew side by side, virtually wing-tip to wing-tip.

The Americans had two air-gunners in their Avengers and left the pilot to do all the navigating, but we had an observer, so my position was in the rear cockpit.

We took off and did our exercises without any issues, but, as we came back to land, one of the two wheels got stuck in the undercarriage and wouldn't come down. The pilot flew around and gave the Avenger a good shake, but the wheel still wouldn't budge. He said that he'd have to land the plane on one wheel, and he told us to prepare ourselves for that.

He took the plane down and did a great job in keeping it balanced on the single wheel after touching down. However, as we slowed, the plane lost its balance and tipped over to one side, causing a wing to touch the ground and sparks to shoot up. The wing was taken off and we were spun around, but the plane came to a standstill and we were able to climb out without further ado.

The nearest town to our airfield was Campbeltown, which was four or five miles by road. I took the bus into town to go to a dance. I had a good drink, but I missed the last bus and had no choice but to make my own way back. As I walked out of the town onto the B-road that led to the base, I could see the lights of the airfield in the distance. Rather than do the sensible and stay on the road, which had a lot of twists and turns, I decided that it would be quicker to hike in a straight line over the fields.

I had only been walking a minute or two when I stumbled and fell into a ditch. I'd had a fair few drinks, so I decided to lay there for a while and rest. I woke up wet through, and managed to find my way back to camp. I was too tired to get undressed, so I got into bed in my soaking wet clothes and slept in them.

As part of the training, we continued to take part in night flying exercises, which I wasn't so keen on. These started about six o'clock in the evening when the first two crews went up. They did their exercises and, on their return, the next pair of planes went up. This continued throughout the night.

One night, early in the exercises, I was in the last pair of planes to take off at around five o'clock in the morning. It was dark and there was no moonlight, but we did our routines and landed safely. I hung around to wait for the other plane to come in, but it never arrived. It had to be assumed that they had gone into the sea and that the three crew members were lost. Nobody knows what happened, but it may have been that they failed to pull out in time when carrying out one of the dive-bombing exercises that were always a bit nerve-racking.

I went to the mess room and had to give the other crew members the news. The response was typically sober and muted.

A few days later, after another night flying exercise, we stopped on the runway and an armourer came out to take away the shells and other ammunition that hadn't been used. I asked him whether he wanted any help to put them back into the armoury, but he said that he could manage by himself. As he walked away from me, I called after him to say that the safety pins hadn't been put back in. He shrugged his shoulders as if to say, 'So what?'

Two days later, there was a huge explosion in the armoury. Three chaps were killed outright and three others injured, one so badly that he died a few hours later.

With the crew of the plane that had gone down a few days previously, we had lost seven people in a very short space of time without the enemy doing a thing. That's often how it was in the war – plenty of people were killed by accidents rather than in action.

Of the thirty air-gunners who had passed out with us in Canada, six of them were lost within six months. It had hit me hard when Henry was killed, but we began to accept that this was how it was going to be.

We knew that if the war went on for too much longer, our chances of survival were not good. There were times when I thought that there was no way that I would get through it, and that I should do my best to live for each day at a time.

JAMES PITTS

CHAPTER TEN

Later that summer, we were moved on to Northern Ireland to continue our training at two small aerodromes, RNAS Maydown and RNAS Eglinton, both of which were close to Lough Foyle and not far from the border with the Republic of Ireland. Here, we were given training in how to oppose U-boats and how to conduct convoy escort duties.

The number of aircrew at the bases was continually changing as they moved people around, and often we had more crew than planes (something that was further accentuated when they reduced the number of Avengers in our squadron in preparation for conversion to a 'composite' unit that would also contain a fighter complement). This meant that it was possible, should one have wanted it, to sit out some of the exercises and operations, but nobody was willing to do that because we each felt that we had to accept our share of the risks. You asked yourself how you would feel if somebody went up in your place and was lost? Nobody wanted to be called a coward, and we'd have rather risked our lives than have anybody say that about us.

In September, a couple of weeks before my twentieth birthday, we were moved to Bangor to board HMS Premier[36] in Belfast Lough. The pilots didn't come with us because they stayed behind to fly the aircraft from Eglinton the following day. Their arrival brought the squadron's complement up to twenty-four officers and twelve ratings, although at different times there would be up to fifty of us on the carrier. Including the air maintenance crew, there was around one hundred of us in total, and, because we shared a crew room, we enjoyed a certain familiarity. We were told to address the officers as 'sir'; but whenever the squadron and ship commanders weren't around we tended to call them by their first names. The commanders frowned on this familiarity, but the officers seemed to have no issue with it.

My pilot was a chap named Baboneau, who that summer had been given two weeks' leave to get married and who came from a family that was involved in an orchestra. He was a very intelligent man, but he could be a bit temperamental and I was never sure as to which mood I'd find him in.

The pilots had to do their first flying from the carrier, and we quickly learned that taking off was quite a trick, while the landing was even more of a challenge. The carrier wasn't allowed to show floodlights, and all there was to guide the plane back was a small light between five and six degrees. If the pilot failed to pick that up, he had to go around until he did, and if he didn't pick it up then he ended up in the sea.

The pilots were required to do their first four test flights on their own, with the observer and air-gunner being excused on the basis that, should the plane go down, only one man would be lost rather than three.

It was my responsibility to ensure that the pilot's radio was tuned into the correct frequency for contact with the ship. I set the radio, bade him well and left him to get on with it. I returned to the crew room, where it suddenly dawned on me that

I had set him on the wrong channel. Aware of him being highly strung and likely to panic, I sprinted back to the deck, where I saw the plane at the end of the flight deck. Making sure that he didn't see me, I jumped into the back of the plane and switched the frequency over. Before I could get back out, the plane took off!

Not wanting to be called out for my mistake, I kept my head down as he flew around. He landed the plane safely, but I thought to myself, 'I'm not doing this three more times' and I jumped out.

However, I was spotted by somebody in the control tower, and all hell broke loose. There was a lot of shouting and finger-jabbing, and I was put on four charges – leaving the ship without permission, joining the ship without permission, not informing the pilot I was on the plane and unauthorised night flying.

I went back to the crew room, where a little later the pilot came in to announce that, on his fourth landing, he had hit the barrier and written off the plane, although he had not been hurt.

I must have looked a big glum because he said to me, 'What's the matter, Jim?' I replied, 'I've just been put on a charge – unauthorised night flying.' He said, 'Who have you been flying with?' I told him, 'You!' He thought I was pulling his leg, but once I'd convinced him that it was true he saw the funny side of it.

I was taken before the ship's commander and ordered to explain myself. Everybody spoke up for me, and the commander of the aircrew asked for the charges to be dismissed. But the ship commander wouldn't have it, and, as far as he was concerned, I had left the ship without permission. He insisted that I had to be punished, although he gave me the minimum sanction that he could impose, which was to postpone me getting my hook back for another month. I had been only a few days from getting it again.

Something I didn't know at the time was that this meant I should not have been allowed back into a plane. Because of my punishment, I was a Naval Airman One and, officially, you needed a rank in case you were taken prisoner.

I wasn't the only person to be up on a charge in front of that commander.

The planes were kept secure on the flight deck with the help of wooden chocks placed against the wheels — as the plane was about to take off, the chock man's job was to pull the blocks away. During a take-off, one of these chaps got blown over the side into the sea.

They sent a cutter out to pick him up, but he used the chocks as flotation aids and made his way back to the ship. Once he was back on it, he was put on a charge of leaving the ship without permission and joining the ship without permission! It didn't help his cause that when the cutter came back to the ship, it made a right mess of the docking and caused some damage.

The flight deck was only four hundred and forty feet in length, which meant that it wasn't long enough for the planes to stop of their own accord when landing. The ship was fitted with arrester wires the width of the flight deck, the idea being that the pilot dropped a hook to catch on the wires, which pulled the plane up before the safety nets.

After one anti-submarine exercise, we came into land, but, because it was a bad landing, the pilot decided to go around again. However, the hook got caught on a safety barrier just as the plane accelerated. We jumped the first safety barrier and went through the second to collide with two planes — we took the wing off one and the tail off another and finished on our nose, dangling over the edge of the flight deck.

I was afraid that the plane might catch fire so I got ready to jump out, but the ship's crew ran up to me, waving their arms and shouting, 'Don't jump, don't jump!' If I had, I'd have dropped straight into the sea.

All three planes were written off, with all operational parts salvaged before the planes were tipped into the sea. These were certainly not the only planes to be damaged beyond repair during such exercises. Another plane hit a barrier and was written off after its hook failed to come down, while one pilot had the distinction of hitting the barrier twice in eight days, although him and his crew walked away from both crashes with barely a scratch. Such was the number of incidents that replacement aircraft had to be flown onto the ship before we could see our first action.

JAMES PITTS

CHAPTER ELEVEN

With all the mishaps that we had experienced, it was no surprise that the carrier had to go into the Clyde shipyard at Greenock, near Glasgow, for repairs. We were given eight days' leave, so I took a troop train to London and went to a dance. I got chatting to a policeman who told me that his parents lived in Glasgow, and he said that I should visit them on my way back to the ship. They lived in Sauchiehall Street, one of the most notorious streets in the city.

When I got to Glasgow, I knocked on their door. It turned out the father was also a policeman, as were most of his relatives. They took me out drinking, and that was the first time that I got into Teacher's Whisky. I got so drunk that, when we went back to their house for a nightcap, I was sick several times in their toilet. I had no idea how I made it back to the ship.

We put to sea and made our way to Scapa Flow,[37] in the Orkney Islands, where a lot of work had been carried out to make it as secure as possible from German attacks. It was well positioned for the ships that patrolled the North Atlantic and Arctic waters, and was within striking distance of the Norwegian coast and the fjords, where there was plenty of

German activity on land, sea and air right up until the end of the war[38].

My first operational flight from the Premier was a mine-laying run up the Karmsund narrows near Haugesund and to the north of Stavanger, which was a city of strategic importance to the Germans and which we were informed was heavily defended.

The operation was named 'Handfast' and the plan was to mine the narrow strip of water to make it impossible for the German ships to navigate it, thus forcing them out into the sea, where our submarines and ships were better placed to pick them up.

We were one of nine Avengers and four Wildcats to set off from the Premier, while we were given support by additional Wildcats from another carrier, HMS Pursuer. The idea was that we would fly into the narrows in formation and drop the mines in a predetermined pattern that would make it difficult for the Germans to sweep for them. One would come alive on the first day and thereafter one each on the following days.

We were given a briefing by our commander, who said that we had to be in formation at one hundred and fifty feet above the water's surface when we released the mines. He stressed that we had to make sure that the mines landed only in the water — should anybody get it wrong and drop one onto land, the resulting explosion would be of sufficient strength to wipe out us all.

The carrier got to around one hundred miles off the coast, and then we did our bit.

The mine was a heavy piece of equipment, weighing some fifteen hundred pounds. At take-off, as the plane left the flight deck, the extra weight of the mine caused the plane to drop towards the sea. We seemed to almost touch the water before we were able to start climbing. Mind you, it was a good idea to stay low in the hope that the Germans wouldn't pick us up and send their fighter planes out to intercept us.

We were all nerves but trying not to show it as we got into formation on our approach to the target, the planes flying three abreast in three lines, our wing tips within a few feet of those of the planes on either side of us. The Avengers had a wingspan of around forty-five feet – imagine three of them going side-by-side up a stretch of water not much wider than the Thames in the centre of London. There was no margin for error, and I spent a good deal of my time watching to see whether we were going to clip the wing of the next plane.

As soon as the mine was released the plane was a lot lighter – it wanted to jerk up about fifteen feet. To me, sitting in the rear, it seemed inevitable that we would collide with another plane's wing, and this was something that I found more disconcerting than anything that was to happen to me later on the Arctic Convoys. However, our pilots did a great job in avoiding contact, and perhaps they should have had been considered for a career in the Red Devils!

All we wanted to do was get back to the relative safety of the ship, but what happened next was something that the pilots had not expected. We got down the narrow straight of water, covering a distance of about sixty miles, and prepared to head back out to sea when the air currents tossed us around. We had to reassemble, and we ended up crossing the coast near to an aerodrome at Stavanger, where the Germans had some fighter planes. We were spotted, and they sent up flak, which missed our plane but which did shatter the windscreen of another Avenger, temporarily blinding the pilot. The enemy scrambled a few Messerschmitts to chase us, but we made it back to the ship and the Germans called off the pursuit without getting to fire on us.

A week later, we received a signal from the Commander in Chief of the Home Fleet reporting an unusually large

concentration of enemy shipping in ports and anchorage between Stavanger and Kristiansand, around one hundred miles
along the coast from Stavanger, which they attributed to our
mine-laying exercise having disrupted their shipping patterns.

Between operations, when the ship was anchored offshore, we
had plenty of free time. Outside of meal times, the aircrew room
was used to put on classes for any of the chaps that wanted to
take part. Rather than spend my time idling around, I signed up
for all the language courses – for a brief spell I was learning four
different languages!

When calm, the water was crystal clear, and, on one
glorious day, I looked over the bow to see shoals of fish
swimming close to the surface. I obtained a length of wire
and string to make an improvised fishing line that I lowered into
the water. I didn't have any bait, but the fish seemed to be
attracted to the shine of the wire and I landed eight or nine fish
in just a few minutes. They were a type of sole, so I took them
down to the galley, where a cook pan-fried them in butter. They
were a nice contrast to the typical ship fare, and I shared them
with the other members of the aircrew, which made me quite
popular.

For our next exercise, we set off from Scapa Flow for a proposed
'beat up' of the Norwegian coast, but, after a day at sea, we ran
into the most terrific storm, the waves being taller than the flight
deck, which was sixty feet high.

As the gale blew, so the crew scrambled to take the planes into
the hanger to lash them down. However, the wind speeds picked
up to over sixty knots (seventy miles per hour), and one plane
had to be left out on the flight deck, where the crew lashed it
down as best they could.

We went down to the mess deck, but the weight of the water

coming over the flight deck meant that it filtered into the decks below.

I was sitting at a table when somebody dropped a plumb line down from the bulkhead so that we could watch the movement of the ship. We went over twenty degrees to the left and twenty degrees to the right, and I thought to myself, this ship has got no keel, it's flat-bottomed, and how much further than twenty degrees does it need to go before it rolls over?

You had to show that you weren't scared, and there was lots of bravado both on the ship and in the air.

When you were in the plane, it was the threat of going into the sea that was the most troubling because you knew that, should this happen, you had very little chance of survival. I had that same feeling as the ship swayed from side to side, but I told myself that, if it was going to happen, there was nothing I could do about it. We became quite good at managing our emotions.

The storm went on through the night, but it had eased by the morning and we went up to the flight deck. The plane that had been lashed down had vanished – the wave that claimed it was so powerful that it broke the plane's bindings and swept it over the side.

The force of the waves also twisted the girders at the end of the flight deck to the extent that no planes were able to take off. The engineer lieutenant spent the day cutting off the damaged metal and welding on fresh parts.

The Pursuer and HMS The Devonshire, a cruiser, also suffered heavy damage, and, along with our ship and an escort of five destroyers, had to return to Scapa Flow while the remainder of the fleet pressed on for Norway.

Even when there wasn't a storm, the waves were large and the sea was choppy – this wasn't a very forgiving part of the world. You'd be sitting in the aircrew room trying to eat your dinner, and suddenly the plates would shoot down the table and you'd have somebody else's meal in front of you. To help pass the time, we played a lot of cards or board games, but these could be swiftly brought to an end as cards and counters went flying off the table after a high wave or two.

I coped reasonably well with it, but some of the chaps took to their hammocks and pretty much stayed in them until the ship docked!

My way of managing was, at least in part, thanks to the Navy's allocation of rum[39]. We were given a daily tot, with those who didn't want it being given threepence in lieu. A couple of chaps said that they didn't want their tot, so I gave them the money and had their drink.

Each lunchtime, I had three tots of rum, and that is how I coped with life on the carrier – I numbed my senses! For ratings, they mixed each tot of rum with two parts water, although Petty Officers were allowed to have it neat.

This was just one way I found to give myself what I considered to be a slight advantage, which was something we were always on the lookout for.

HMS Premier was one of the smaller carriers with a crew of around five hundred, plus our aircrew of around one hundred.

The living quarters were cramped, and the sleeping quarters were uncomfortable. Our beds were hammocks that were four deep and we had twenty-four men sleeping in a room that wasn't much more than eighteen feet square. The German U-boats were a constant threat, and that meant we had to sleep in our clothes to be ready for anything that may happen, particularly around dusk and dawn, which were the most difficult times to spot the submarines and when they were most likely to come up to attack.

We supposedly had air-conditioning, but this rarely worked. When there was quite a few men sleeping in the room, it would warm up and everybody would be sweating. At times, you could step out of your hammock and put your foot into a puddle of perspiration on the floor. I didn't like that, and I looked for somewhere else to bed down.

Our aircrew room contained lockers for our personal possessions, so it was one of the few rooms where it was possible to lock the door. It was generally quiet at night, so I took my hammock up to the room and laid it out on the floor. I locked the door and tried to sleep, although it wasn't always so easy.

A worrying thought was that the quarters were on the inside of the ship, while all the fuel and ammunition were contained around the exterior. We knew that, should we be hit by a torpedo, everything would go up in one big bang. That played on our nerves a bit because we were aware that it had happened to other carriers of a similar size to ours, but there wasn't anything that I could do about it.

JAMES PITTS

CHAPTER TWELVE

There were some advantages to being part of the aircrew on an aircraft carrier. Each time it docked, we got double leave because there was little reason to keep us on the ship. The ship's crew had to share their leave, with one half retained for operational purposes, so the first watch would go on leave before returning to swap with the second watch. We actually got more than twice their leave, because there was a small overlap.

When the ship docked in Scapa Flow, we were given a week's leave, so I took a drifter over to Thurso, on the mainland, and jumped onto a troop train.

It took twenty-four hours to get to London, and I was soon thinking about getting back to the relative safety of Scapa Flow – the Germans were sending over V-2[40] rockets, which were more frightening even than the V-1s. These made no noise because they travelled faster than the speed of sound, and the first you were aware of them was when there was an explosion. One of the first V-2s landed in Chiswick, killing a couple of people. The Government blamed that incident on a leaking gas main, and it was only a few weeks later, after several other 'unexplained' explosions, that they admitted that the damage was being caused by the V-2s. They had not told the truth because they were concerned about possible panic, but there were too many of these bombs for them to maintain the pretence and they had to tell the truth. Generally, people were pretty stoic and I never came across anybody who made much of a drama about it.

On our return to the ship, we set off with HMS Implacable, HMS Diadem, HMS Trumpeter and eight destroyers for another mine-laying exercise at Karmsund near Haugesund.

We typically went up early in the morning and tried to get into the fjords without stirring the Germans, but that wasn't always possible and this time their gun placements were ready for us. We were accompanied by Wildcats from our own ship and from Trumpeter, who provided cover and challenged the German guns.

We were so low as we flew into the fjord that the Germans were firing down on us from the steep banks at the side of the water. They started by sending tracer bullets at us. This was my first experience of these, and it was unnerving to see these bullets going round and round in circles as they came towards me.

My instinct was to protect my back with the three-quarter inch armour plating that was behind me, but, after a few seconds of indecision, I accepted that I had no option but to turn around and shoot back.

There were bullets flying all over the place, and I had little idea from which direction they were coming. All I could do was aim my gun at where I thought the gun positions were and shoot in that general direction, all the time praying that what the Germans were sending up at us would miss our plane.

I was so tense that the muscles in my hands almost locked on the gun handles and trigger.

We successfully laid the mines and scarpered. We were about forty miles out to sea when we saw one of our Wildcats shot up and drop towards the water. We flew back around and saw it go into the water, but the pilot got out of the plane and into his dinghy. There was nothing we could do for him, and we headed back towards to our ship, which was firing like hell at the Germans to dissuade them from chasing us.

We reported what we had seen, and we were assured that the pilot would be picked up. However, the usual cover provided by the airborne lifeboat was not available for that particular operation due to engine trouble in the RAF Wellington support aircraft, and the pilot was never collected. We never knew what happened to him, but he was lost despite a lengthy search being conducted the following day.

A week later, ours was one of six Avengers from the Premier that, along with eight Wildcats from our carrier and a similar number from Trumpeter, set off to lay mines in one of the main enemy shipping channels off the coast at Ramsund.

We got there without being challenged by any German aircraft, but we were again attacked by their gun positions. This time, they didn't use tracer bullets, and that made it even more difficult to detect their positions. The senior pilot flew alongside us and pointed out the holes in the side of his plane.

We got our fuel calculations wrong and again ended up where we shouldn't have been, which gave the Germans the chance to turn their ack-ack guns on us. They had a fair idea of the height we were flying at, so they were able to set the detonation height accurately. The shells made no noise in the air, and you were only aware of them when you smelt the cordite as one exploded nearby.

When they exploded a little further away, you'd see puffs of smoke. We called this flak, and you didn't want to get too close to it because the metal shards could rip a plane to bits, although on this occasion we all managed to dodge it. All we wanted was to get back to our ship as quickly as possible, and, although six enemy aircraft did get up to chase us, we got close enough to our ship for the anti-aircraft fire to dissuade them from pursuing us further.

Again, we were informed by the C-in-C of the Home Fleet that the operation had been a success.

CHAPTER THIRTEEN

By the middle of December, the weather had taken a huge turn for the worse. We set off on a mine-laying operation that had to be abandoned because of a severe gale that caused substantial damage to the forward end of the flight deck. That gave the engineer lieutenant another lot of work, which was something that he seemed happy to grumble about!

We were again taken back to Scapa Flow, having to pass through another storm that caused the ship to slow its speed considerably. When we finally got there, a replacement Avenger and two Wildcats were flown on, while a deck cargo of damaged aircraft and parts were transferred to the mainland.

The ship headed for the Clyde and further repairs, which was no problem for us because the aircrew were given twelve days' leave. I again caught a troop ship and headed back to London for Christmas.

The V-2s were still causing consternation, and things seemed a little more subdued in the capital compared to my previous visit home.

On our return to the ship, we learned that VHF (very high frequency) radios had been installed in the Avengers. We gave them a thorough testing and were happy enough with them, which meant the end of me and my fellow air-gunners having to communicate via Morse code.

We set off for Scapa Flow and proceeded to sea with Force 3 for Operation Spellbinder. Joining us was Trumpeter, HMS Dido and four destroyers, and we rendezvoused with Force 1, which included HMS Norfolk, HMS Bellona and three more destroyers. Almost immediately enemy aircraft were picked up on the radar. Our Wildcats went up to challenge them, and a German Ju-88 and two Wildcats were lost, although both of our pilots were recovered.

As we concentrated our attention on the battle going on above us, two torpedoes were fired from enemy submarines at the ship, both of which missed.

We withdrew to Scapa Flow, but the next day set off again to Norway for Operation Gratis. Ours was one of seven Avengers from the Premier, and we were joined by a similar number from Trumpeter and a number of covering Wildcats.

Our destination was again Karmsund. We met little opposition and we were able to lay our mines and get away with only very light gun fire to dodge. We had been warned to expect opposition from enemy aircraft, but we got back to the ship without any sign of German planes, which was always a nice feeling.

We prepared for two more mine-laying runs, but each was postponed because of engine problems on the ship. I'm not sure what the issue was, but once it was resolved we set off for another operation, although this one also ran into difficulty as the flight deck became covered in a thick layer of heavy snow. The crew tried their best to clear the deck, but it was an impossible task in the freezing conditions, and, as the snow continued to fall, the operation was cancelled.

This was often the story of the first couple of months of 1945, with snow and ice making it extremely difficult for the ships and aircraft, although we did manage to at least partially mine a shipping channel at Skjoldastraumen. This was another occasion when I spent as much time watching our own planes as I did anything else, for the channel was a very narrow one set between 3,000-feet cliffs. Again, I was more concerned about a collision with one of our own planes or a mine going astray and wiping us out than I was about encountering the Germans. We did the best we could, one plane being unable to drop its mine and another having a serious oil leak, although it managed to get back to the ship.

Because of the number of planes on the carrier, there wasn't sufficient room on the flight deck for the first few planes to take off by themselves. They had to be shot off the carrier by a steam catapult that propelled them along the short deck at such high speed that it took only a couple of seconds for them to get airborne. Taking off this way, the planes reached one hundred miles per hour in around four seconds, but as you cleared the ship your rate of increase slowed considerably and you actually felt as though you were flying backwards, something that I never got used to.

The steam catapult was only good for six take-offs before it had to be recharged, and it was quite a complicated bit of equipment that required regular maintenance. After any sort of maintenance work, you didn't want to be the first plane to take off because, had the catapult not been repaired properly, you ran the risk of not having sufficient velocity to clear the end of the deck correctly, which meant you might drop off the end of the carrier and into the sea.

After one shutdown for repairs, I can't remember which one, there was a discussion among the pilots about who should be first to go up. None of them was particularly keen on being the first to be catapulted off, so they decided to test the instrument by shooting off an upright piano that the officers had in a bar in their ward room. They brought it up to the flight deck, rigged it up and sent the piano flying hundreds of yards out into the sea! Once they were satisfied that the catapult was functioning properly, they were happy to get into their planes.

It was around this time that we were given immersion suits designed to keep the cold away from our bodies for a little longer should we end up in the water. During our training, we had worn warm clothing when flying, nothing special, but these suits were all-in-one rubber outfits that tied up around the neck.

They meant that, instead of lasting only one or two minutes in the water, you might get as long as five minutes. I guess you could say that those extra few minutes may possibly be the most important minutes of your life, although the suits probably wouldn't have been much good to us had we gone into the water – we were normally far from the ship and there wouldn't have been anybody close enough to us to fish us out.

Again, there was a bit of a debate about who was going to be the first to try out the suits by putting them on and being dropped over the side of the ship into the sea. A few chaps put their hand up, and went into the water. There was a general acceptance among crews that you never let one of your pals do something that you could do yourself, but on this occasion I kept my hand down!

All our Avengers were flown to Hatston for further training, although we lost another plane when one was caught in a strong cross wind and cartwheeled onto its back well off the runway. The pilot and his observer had a broken rib or two, while a Wren, who had gone up for a jolly, cut her ear when her head apparently broke through the turret top.

We carried out one further mine-laying operation at a broad stretch of water near Askvoll, meeting little opposition, although the weather had caused yet another delay in us getting airborne.

We returned to Scapa Flow before heading to Greenock and being given a fortnight's leave. We returned to the ship in dry dock at Port Glasgow, and we were told that a reconnaissance photograph of Askvoll had shown a three hundred and seventy-feet Norwegian merchant ship with only its funnel showing above water. The sinking was attributed to our mine-laying run of a couple of weeks previously.

JAMES PITTS

CHAPTER FOURTEEN

On 17th April, we were informed that we were to be part of the escort for Russian convoy JW66,[41] codenamed 'Operation Roundel'.

I'd already had a bit of experience with convoys because on several occasions we had flown out from our bases in Northern Ireland and Scotland to escort ships which had crossed the Atlantic from the United States. We flew up to two hundred miles out to sea to provide cover for the convoys as they came in.

Ahead of setting off for Russia, we had been well briefed about conditions on previous Arctic Convoys, and the officers gave us as much knowledge as they had in their possession. They told us that the Germans had as many as twenty operational U-boats based in the seas around Norway, and that these were supported by as many as one hundred land-based aircraft. Northern Norway, we were told, was the one place left on the planet where the German navy had sufficient forces to continue major operations.

We were told to be under no illusion as to the task in front of us, and it was explained that, although the Germans were taking one hell of a beating on all fronts, they considered attacks on our convoys as 'an essential relief' for its land-based troops as they tried to stop, or at least slow down, the Russian advances on the eastern front.

The previous convoy to ours (JW65) had managed to get in and out of Murmansk without too much trouble from the Germans, but JW64 had been badly beaten up by both U-boats and planes, with several ships sunk or badly damaged. Apparently, the Germans had equipped their U-boats with schnorkels that meant that they could hide themselves away close to the shore and be more of a threat even in the daylight, when it was normally easier for us to pick them up.

We had some advantages in that the Navy was able to read the German's encrypted radio messages and there was the experience garnered from previous convoys.

Ahead of our departure, the officers did their best to get us ready, although I don't think anybody could have been fully prepared for the reality of what Winston Churchill called 'the worst journey in the world'. It was to be an experience beyond anything I had known in my rather young life.

On 18th April, we left Scapa Flow with another carrier, Vindex, the anti-aircraft cruiser Bellona, six destroyers, a few corvettes and a sloop. Our task was to escort twenty-six Merchant Navy ships to Murmansk, the largest city north of the Arctic Circle and one of two destinations for the convoys. As far as I knew, the merchant ships were carrying planes, guns, food and raw materials to help the Russian war effort.

We set off in a northerly direction from Scotland into the Norwegian Sea, where we were joined by a further three destroyers, four corvettes and sixteen Russian submarine chasers out of the Faroe Islands. The plan was to take a turn east to the north of Norway into the Barents Sea and then head down to Murmansk through the Kola inlet (other convoys went to Arkhangelsk, further along the coast, although not in the winter when the ice made the route impassable). Because of the threat posed by the Germans' heavy coastal guns, we kept well out to sea. This also helped to reduce the likelihood of an attack by their planes, although we were on constant watch for them and the German U-boats.

As we passed north of Norway, we had a few scares, with radar contact being made on several occasions with what may have been U-boats. One was eventually judged to be a whale, but another was of sufficient concern that one of the corvettes was sent after it, although there was no contact.

German planes were also detected on radar at ranges of around twenty to thirty miles, bringing us to battle stations, but the contact was lost and we were able to stand down.

If there wasn't too much to report in terms of action, in terms of the weather it was a different experience altogether. In spite of it being (allegedly) spring, the winds were strong and the seas rough, there was a heavy swell with regular, and often heavy, snow showers. I was grateful for my tots of rum whenever we went up on patrol.[42]

The temperature at five thousand feet was as low as minus forty degrees Fahrenheit (-40°C), although we later met up with other squadrons who told us that we had no cause for complaint because they'd had to endure temperatures of minus sixty degrees on their convoys!

Because of the threat from beneath the seas and in the skies, our planes, as well as those from HMS Vindex, were required to be on patrol around the clock.

Each crew's patrol lasted four hours at a time, with alternating day and night duty, and we had to fly a set pattern over a wide area to scan for possible submarines. The maximum height the plane could fly to was around ten thousand feet, but, for all intents and purposes, we'd typically be at five thousand to six thousand feet because that gave us the best angle to try to spot the submarines, even though this was something of a thankless task.

We had been given training in how to use our eyes to scan large areas. We would look down at the huge expanse of water and try to pick out a periscope or a rising submarine, but it was like trying to pick out a needle in a haystack. After a short spell of intense concentration, your eyes began to hurt and you felt dizzy. You'd be seeking out a speck of colour or movement, anything slightly out of the ordinary, and we had a mine ready to drop on anything we did see, but the likelihood of spotting a U-boat was minimal, and I certainly didn't manage it.

Because our planes covered such a large area, often a hundred miles or more away from the convoy, at the back of our minds was the concern that we would not be able to find our way back to our carrier. The threat of attracting unwanted attention from the enemy meant that the ship could not send out much of a signal for us to track, so it was pretty much up to the three of us to work our way back, which, for me, meant that our observer was the most important man in the entire war effort! Once you got closer to the ship, you might pick up a weak signal, but we had been made aware of crews on previous convoys who had not managed to detect a signal and who had circled round and round looking for their ship until they ran out of fuel and were lost.

The further north we proceeded in the direction of the Arctic, the more uncomfortable our experience became.

As we turned into the Barents Sea, not too far from Bear Island, we were around seventy-five minutes into a patrol when we spotted that ice had formed on the wings of our plane. It was about half-an-inch thick, but the longer we were in the air the thicker it became.

The ice thickened to about two inches and, without warning, the engine cut out – the fuel must have frozen. We dropped towards the sea, and the three of us, completely helpless, knew that, even should we survive the initial contact with the water, we'd be gone within minutes in the cold, even allowing for the fact that we were wearing our new immersion suits.

The plane continued to fall for seemingly an age and we said our goodbyes to each other, trying our best to not be too emotional about it, but, when we got to within one thousand feet of the sea, or maybe less, the pilot somehow got the engine going again. He pulled the plane up, and the three of us gave a mighty cheer!

The observer said something like, 'Thank God for that – let's go back to the carrier.' But the pilot said, 'No, we'll finish our patrol.' I had no say in the matter. For another two and a half hours, we were up in the dark sky, watching the ice build up again on the wing, with me and the observer asking the pilot to at least take the plane to a lower level, where the air temperature wasn't quite so severe.

That was one of my worst experiences of the war, worse than all the crashes. When you've got time to think about what your likely destiny is going to be, that's not so good. But it turned out okay for us, and we had to think how fortunate we had been.

Each time a plane took off or landed, the carrier was required to move out of the convoy. Taking off from a carrier was very different to taking off from land – because of the shortness of the flight deck we needed to get as much air as possible over the wings to assist lift-off, which meant that the ship needed to be heading into the wind and in the direction of take-off.

When landing, you couldn't come at the ship in a straight line. You flew around the carrier and turned and banked so that you came in at an angle – this helped to produce the minimum landing speed. The pilots had been given plenty of training to help them manage this technique, but it wasn't easy, especially in such difficult weather conditions, and a couple of planes crashed as they attempted their landings, although nobody was lost.

Between each four-hour patrol, we had twenty-four hours during which we had no duties other than to look after the aircraft. We sometimes went to the front of the ship, where the parachutes were packed. The packers made us cups of tea and seemed pleased to have us around. We'd go up the ladder to the galley in the afternoon, and the cooks were also nice to us – they'd make us egg and chips, ham and chips, whatever we asked for. There was a reason for this: because of our briefings, we always knew where the ship was heading and what the orders were. They didn't, so they gave us food in exchange for information!

They made us lovely sandwiches to take onto the plane when we went on patrol. One of the cooks went to the flight deck to watch each time a plane took off. I asked him why, and he said, 'Just in case you come down – I'd like to see that'!

We had no further contact with the enemy until we approached Kola Inlet, which would lead us down to Murmansk. Here, the convoy was vulnerable to the packs of U-boats which were relentlessly hunting for us, and we were called to battle stations. We were told that there was a number of U-boats stalking the entrance to Kola Inlet and that we would probably have to force our way into Murmansk.

Our patrols were increased to help screen the merchant ships, with us sometimes going ahead of the convoy to drop sonar buoys, while at other times we patrolled the flanks. As we made our way into the inlet, so the ships dropped depth charges at random. Most of us were a little nervous as we waited for signs of a German attack, and several times contacts were chased which turned out to be no more than shoals of fish!

We passed through a minefield that had been laid ahead of us in an attempt to thwart the U-boats, and we arrived at the port at Murmansk on 25th April without any attack from the enemy submarines, and with the only damage done to our carrier being the result of our own exercises and the inclement weather.

JAMES PITTS

CHAPTER FIFTEEN

The Soviet authorities seemed to be very wary of us, and we were given orders as to how to behave and where to go (and where not to go) in the city. We weren't told exactly when we would set off on the return journey because our officers were busy monitoring the movements of the enemy U boats and planes as they put together a plan to try to deceive them.

The ship got up a football team to take on the locals, and, after a bit of negotiation, the game was allowed to go ahead. I wasn't selected for our team, but that was no surprise because I wasn't really into football. Some of the officers and ratings from the destroyers also performed a concert at the Red Navy Club at Polyarnoye, at the mouth of the Kola inlet, as they waited there for the return convoy to be formed.

I went with a couple of pals for a walk around Murmansk,[43] but it was a grim place that had been horribly scarred by the war. I had thought that we were poor in England, especially compared to what I had seen in New York and at other bases in the United States and Canada, but poverty had been taken to a new level here.

We stopped outside a baker's shop, where there was a queue of women doing their best to ignore the freezing cold, and we watched as each customer had their ration weighed out in turn – all they received were three or four crusts of what seemed to barely pass for bread.[44] Their clothing was very poor and several of them were wrapped in what appeared to be rags to protect themselves as best they could from the biting winds and bitter temperatures.

As we walked around the streets, a soldier approached us and showed us some knives with fancy handles. He indicated that he wanted to us to buy them from him. They looked quite nice and I might have been tempted, but, before we had time to make an offer, a guard came rushing over and pointed his gun at the man. He led him away at the end of his rifle.

There seemed to be a lot of suspicion, people appeared reluctant to meet your eyes, and it was quite clear that the authorities had done nothing to encourage their people to mix with us. It wasn't the fault of ordinary people, but I wondered whether those outside the docks understood what we were doing and why we were in their city.

There was only one restaurant that was open, and we decided to go into it to have a look at what was on offer. However, the food looked less appetising than that on the ship and we were suspicious of its origins, so we agreed to give it a pass.

We didn't venture too much further than the port itself, so I can't speak for the city as a whole. We found a small dance hall and went in to see that a couple of tables had been reserved for the men from the convoys.

However, there was no alcohol available for purchase, only soft drinks, and the people again didn't seem keen to make eye contact or to converse with us. Sitting close to the door were a couple of men in uniform who seemed to have an air of authority about them, and we surmised that anybody who tried to get friendly with us might well have to explain themselves to these men, and who knew where that may lead them. It was easier for us to have a quick drink and get back to the ship.

We were briefed that we had twenty-two merchant ships to escort back to Britain, most of these having come in on the convoy ahead of ours. However, getting out into the Barents Sea was going to be a bit tricky because our chaps had picked up that a dozen U-boats were laying in wait off the Kola Inlet. The Germans knew where we were, and they were obviously aware that we had to come out.[45]

To try to trick the Germans into thinking that we were to depart on the night of 27th April, the Russians were asked to turn on a number of lights and to send anti-submarine vessels into the inlet to drop depth charges, while our ships sent out dummy radio signals suggesting that we were shortly to be on the move.

The enemy apparently did not fall for the ruse, so it was repeated again the following night, again without success. On the night of 29th April we finally headed out of the port and into the inlet, all the time aware that we were likely to encounter the enemy in the very near future.

Four escorts led the way and quickly found a U-boat, which they attacked and which went down stem first. A few minutes later there was a huge explosion as HMS Goodall, a frigate, was hit by a homing torpedo that caused its armoury to explode and the ship to immediately take on water.[46]

Suddenly, it was like the biggest firework display you'd ever seen.

HMS Honeysuckle, a corvette, went to the Goodall to help evacuate the crew, but it was damaged by the explosion and had to draw off.

The escort ships threw out mines as quickly as they could, dozens of them, as torpedoes went speeding through the water, and there was a huge amount of noise, light and confusion.

The convoy broke up as the frigates went hunting for the U-boats, and at least one more submarine was sunk. Our planes could not take off from the carriers while we were in the inlet, so we had to stay on the ship and watch the melee.

All aircrew were on battle stations, standing next to our planes to tackle any emergency which may arise, but we could only get into the air once the carrier was facing into the wind, and we had to wait until we were out at sea for it to turn to face the necessary direction.

The Russians sent up their planes from nearby airfields, and the Soviet chasers and our escorts continued to mix it with the U-boats, dropping depth-charges whenever and wherever they could.

We got out of the inlet without our ship being damaged and we took our planes up into the air with mines attached. We went hunting for the U-boats without managing to spot any as they sloped away.

As things calmed down, we finally returned to the carrier. The ship commander came to the aircrew room to inform us that, while we were in the air, the carrier had had a grand total of six torpedoes fired at her, although they had all missed.

This was to be the last convoy battle of the war, and the Goodall was the last major British warship to be sunk by the Germans. Nearly one hundred men died, including the commander, with only a handful of survivors taken out of the water.

We got out into the open sea, but we remained on battle stations and continued our round-the-clock patrols because we had been made aware that the convoy was being shadowed by reconnaissance aircraft.

With so much activity, there was always going to be the potential for mishaps, and two planes on their return from patrols went into the barrier on landing, while another plane was so badly covered in ice that it stalled on its approach and crashed onto the deck, where it burst into flames. Fortunately, the ship's crew got the fire out quickly, although the pilot was hurt quite badly. The observer and air-gunner managed to walk off the wing having escaped serious injury.

The plane was damaged to the extent that it was pushed off the side of the ship into the sea. This was something that I witnessed on several occasions, although only after the write-offs had been stripped of any usable parts, especially their engines.

We had no further contact with the U-boats and, while at sea, we were informed of the death of Adolf Hitler. We had no idea how the German crews would react to that news, and the officers insisted that we were still at war and to act accordingly.

Our last patrol was on 7th May, and this proved to be the last patrol of the Russian Convoys in wartime. There were no incidents to report, and my pilot landed our plane successfully at around two-thirty in the morning.

We broke away from the convoy to return to Scapa Flow, and docked on 8th May to the news that Germany had surrendered and that the war in Europe was finally over.

We had quite a drink-up to celebrate that news. Ordinary ratings like me weren't allowed to drink beer on the ship, but the officers brought us jugs of beer, and the pilots gave us mugs of beer. The rum was also brought out.

We got a drifter to take us to the airbase bar, which was open only for a couple of hours each afternoon. One of the cooks made a late decision to join us and came jogging up as the drifter was pushing away from the ship. He jumped for it, but landed awkwardly and broke a leg. We went to the bar while he went to hospital. Other squadrons came back, and we met up with mates who had been on other ships and who we hadn't seen for some time. It was some drink-up!

The beer was terrible, but we downed as much as we could before we had to get back on the drifter to return to the ship. There were up to two hundred people crowded onto the small boat whose sides were only eighteen inches or so above the water. The sea was a bit rough, so quite a few of the chaps made the trip with their head over the side being sick. One of the chaps leaned too far over the edge and fell in, and we had to stop to fish him out. When the drifter arrived at the ship, because the sea was choppy we had to jump for the gangway. Again, one or two fell in and had to be pulled out.

The next day we disembarked to Hatston, thus ending our association with Premier, and it was from there that I got to drop my only mines of the war. Some of the German U-boats that had been surrendered were brought to Scapa Flow, and we had some fun flying up to drop mines on them.

856 Squadron was disbanded on 15th June, having been in existence for some sixteen months. Some of those chaps I did not see again for fifty years. Others I never saw again.

CHAPTER SIXTEEN

After my squadron was disbanded, I was ordered to the Fleet Air Arm base at Lee-on-the-Solent,[47] near Portsmouth, Hampshire, and put on standby to go out to the Far East as a replacement air-gunner – the war with Japan was still being fiercely fought and it looked like it could be going on for some time.

I was put on a few hours' notice to depart, with all my kit packed, and it stayed that way until VJ Day was announced two months later. Like everybody else, I couldn't believe what the A-bombs had done to Hiroshima and Nagasaki,[48] but, having got through the war in Europe, I was mightily relieved that I didn't have to go to fight another war in Asia.

Indeed, I felt fortunate to have survived at all because there had been times during the preceding couple of years when I had honestly believed that seeing out the war would be beyond me.

We got so drunk on VJ Day, the entire country seemed to be celebrating. We went to a nearby pub and had the drink-up to beat all drink-ups. People were just so happy and relieved, there was a massive release of tension. I got so drunk that I could not recall returning to our billet, and when I woke up in my bed the next morning I was still fully dressed. I noticed that one of our chaps had not come back – his bed was unmade. I asked around to find out where he was, and I was told that he was in Haslar hospital.[49] Apparently, in high spirits and with a belly full of alcohol, he had taken a fire engine from the company fire station and driven it out of the camp and down the road. He had crashed it and concussed himself, although, thankfully, nobody else had been hurt.

I went to the hospital to see him, and, as soon as I walked into his room, he said to me, 'Do you fancy a drink, Jim?' He put on his dressing gown, called a couple of nurses to come with us, and we walked out of the hospital. We went down the street and into a pub with him in his dressing gown and a couple of nurses in uniform, which earned us some funny looks. I said to him that he was going to get the book thrown at him, but he talked his way out of it.

We had another good drink. On our return to the hospital, we got talking to an air-gunner who had only recently arrived there, having been held as a prisoner-of-war by the Germans. He told us that his plane had been shot down by a Messerschmitt and that he had bailed out over the Norwegian coast. His parachute had opened okay, but he was blown all over the place and he survived only by holding on for grim life to the edge of a cliff before being captured. He had a scar on his chest where he had been hit by a bullet. His experiences had obviously affected him, and I don't think they were too keen to let him out. He was among a group of thirty to forty former prisoners-of-war who were taken back to Lee-on-the-Solent in the time that I was there.

I sat a few exams and was made a Petty Officer, and I surprised myself at how I took to the role. I had felt myself to be a bit of a jack-the-lad, a bit independent of thought and deed, but once I had that responsibility thrust on me I began to change my outlook and attitude.

Not that I got everything right. After being kept awake all night by a painful toothache, the following morning I was the right-hand marker for a division, which meant that I had to basically march with a line of men following behind me. The idea was that I would turn right on instruction and the men would reform behind me, but, being only half awake and trying to ignore the throbbing pain in my mouth, I turned left instead of right. Pandemonium broke out behind me. The men didn't know which way to turn and the line became a shambles, like something out of a comedy film.

The Chief Petty Officer got quite cross and he ordered me to fall out. He demanded to know why somebody of my rank and experience had made such a novice mistake. I explained that I was in a lot of pain because of the toothache, and, to my surprise, he was actually reasonably sympathetic and did no more than tell me to report to the dentist.

I went to the dental surgery, which was in a house close to the base. The surgeon was a commander with three rings on his sleeve. I told him that I wanted the tooth taken out, to which he replied, 'See these three rings – they give me the right to tell you what you'll have done, and you'll have done what I tell you.' He told me to get into the chair, and he proceeded to inspect my teeth. He said that, in spite of what I had requested, he was prepared to only fill the tooth, which was towards the rear of my mouth. However, after a lot of drilling, he said that the tooth was in worse shape than he had initially thought and that he would put in a temporary filling and do further work at another time. He told me to return in three weeks for him to insert a permanent filling, but I was given orders to take a draft of seven men to Arbroath to form a new squadron and I left before the appointment.

We took the train from Portsmouth to London, where we had

a few hours to wait before taking a connecting train northwards. I had to arrange for all the kit to be transferred between the different stations, and that took up quite a lot of time. One of the chaps, a young man, said to me, 'I live not far from here – could I go and visit my wife for a couple of hours?' I had been given orders not to let anyone out of my sight, and I told him, sorry, but I can't let you go. He looked so crestfallen that I relented and said to him, 'Okay, you can go, but you have to promise me that you'll come back to catch the train.' He gave me his word, and he kept it.

I was the senior air-gunner on the squadron in Arbroath. People were starting to be demobbed, and I had to think about what I wanted to do. Your previous employer was obliged to keep your job open for you, and I knew I could go back to Sperry's, but I thought that I might like to stay in the Navy and make a career for myself.

For those who wanted out but didn't have a trade, the Navy laid on training courses, and quite a few men did bricklaying or woodwork courses, got some qualifications and left to become brickies or chippies.

People were being let go according to their age and length of service. I was called into the office and informed that I was to be demobbed. I told my squadron's lieutenant commander that I would be leaving the following week, and he asked me whether that was what I wanted. 'I don't think so,' I told him. He said to leave it with him and to carry on as I was, which is what I did.

Shortly before Christmas, I was called in again and asked what I was doing still at the base because I should have already departed. I explained that the lieutenant commander had okayed it for me to stay on, but they said, 'You can't just stay on like that – you've got to sign on for a specific amount of time. There's no way you can stay on and think that you can leave when you feel like it.' They offered me a choice of signing on for another year, which they said they wanted me to do, or to leave before the end of the year.

I decided to get out, primarily because the planes we had been given were Barracudas.[50] These were dive-bombers, terrible planes, nobody liked them, and I couldn't get used to them. I had thought the Swordfish a smashing plane, and the Avenger was fine, but the Barracuda had a reputation for crashing and there had been a problem with pilots being made unconscious by leaks from the hydraulics.

That autumn, a lot of senior engineers had been demobbed, which had left mostly junior engineers to look after the planes. Whether it was a lack of expertise, a lack of experience or simply that the planes weren't up to the task, I don't know, but three planes went down in three months with nine men lost.

Among those was the young air-gunner to whom I had given permission to sneak away for a few hours while we were travelling through London. It was a little consolation for me to know that I had bent the rules and at least given him a last time with his wife. Who knows, a new life could have been conceived in those few hours.

I went up in a Barracuda with a pilot who was a bit of a show-off. He put us into a steep dive and left it very late to pull out. He told me that he was going to repeat the exercise, but I told him that we should go back. We had a bit of a tiff, but I got my way. After we landed, we saw a gaping hole in one of the wings which had obviously occurred as we had pulled out of the dive.

This was why these planes were being lost – they couldn't take the stress. They had to tell the pilots to stop putting the planes into steep dives, which rather defeated the object of having them. I didn't like the odds being offered by the Barracudas, so I decided to leave the service.

With nowhere else to go, I headed back to London and Dad's house.

Unfortunately, my aching tooth was never properly sorted out while I was in service, and, after having a nagging toothache for several days, it became so painful that, at nine o'clock in the evening, I knocked on the door of a dentist and pleaded with him to extract it. He took me into his surgery and removed the tooth, giving me a bill for ten shillings and six pence (52.5p in modern money).

Dad had set himself up as a small building company, employing a labourer to work with him, while Nell had given birth to another daughter, Christine. I moved back into their home in Ealing, but they didn't really have enough space for me and their growing family, so I moved out again.

I found lodgings in St Stephen's Road, Hounslow, then nearby Roseville Avenue, where I lived for the next eight years. I also went back to work at Sperry's. The war department that I had previously worked in had been shut down, so I returned to the company as a Capstan setter.

Above: James (left) as a telegraphist air-gunner. He is pictured with his pilot and observer

Below: The flightdeck of HMS Premier

Above: The ships of the Arctic Convoys had to contend with treacherous conditions on their journey through freezing seas

Left: The convoys delivered a variety of supplies to the Soviet Union

Right: The convoys made their way from Britain to the Soviet Union's northern ports

Above: The aircraft carrier HMS Premier

Below: James trained in a Swordfish (the air-gunner was in the rear seat)

Above: James married Dianne in 1956

Below: James and Dianne with their three sons in 1965

Left: James in the city of Arkhangelsk in 2005. It was his first trip back to Russia since the convoys

Above: James (right) giving Tony Blair, the Prime Minister, an ear-bashing during a reception at 10 Downing Street

Right: Cdr Eddie Grenfell fought a tireless campaign to have convoy veterans awarded the Arctic Star

Above and below: James with fellow veterans and dignitaries aboard HMS Belfast on the River Thames in London

Above and below: James and Charles Downs represented Britain by carrying the Olympic Flame in Arkhangelsk in 2013

Above: James marching at the Cenotaph for the final time in memory of Cdr Eddie Grenfell

Below: James makes a point to General David Richards during a function on HMS Belfast

James and some of the veterans at the impressive Museum of the Great Patriotic War in Moscow to hand over his Arctic Star medal. James gave a speech before passing the medal to the museum's director, Vladimir Zaborovskiy

Above: James was guest of honour at a function at the House of Lord's organised by the Friends of North Caucasus

Below: James, who celebrated his ninetieth birthday in 2014, has been married to Dianne since 1956

CHAPTER SEVENTEEN

I had qualified for some war medals, but I didn't see the need to collect them. The war was over, I had returned to civilian life, and I felt it best to put it all behind me and get on with the rest of my life. The medals weren't important to me, and I didn't see how they would benefit me.

Many of the chaps who had served had a similar attitude – it was the done thing not to talk about the war, we felt that we should move on and earn our living. Sperry's was, hopefully, my future and the war was something that I'd rather not trouble myself about.

Five or six years later, the Navy announced that it had some prize-money for anybody who had served during the war. It had sold some of the German ships which had been captured, and there was a bounty to be shared, which was between eighteen and twenty pounds per person. I thought that was worth having, it being roughly what I earned in a fortnight!

To receive the money, you were asked to claim your medals at the same time. I was given four medals – the 1939-1945 Star (for service at sea), the Atlantic Star (for service in the Atlantic, for which the qualification was a minimum of six months), the

War Medal (for being in the services for a minimum of a month) and the Defence Medal (for serving abroad for a year, or something like that).

I was given the medals in a box along with a bit of paper explaining what they were for. I left them in that box for the next forty-five years, and only got them out in 1995 when my three sons got on at me after the Government decided that it needed to mark the fiftieth anniversary of the end of the war in Europe.

Sperry's moved some of its business from Brentford to Feltham, a little further to the west going away from the centre of London, and I went to work there. One of the chaps I worked with, Bill, had lodgings with a family in Sunbury-on-Thames, which was a couple of miles from the factory. They had a house party, to which I was invited. I got talking to the daughter of the woman who owned the house, Dianne Livermore, but she was seeing another chap and she said that they were soon to get engaged.

Bill rode a motorbike, and he had an accident that saw him taken to West Middlesex Hospital, Isleworth. I went to visit him, and Dianne turned up at the same time. Bill was in a bit of a mess and Dianne was upset, so I walked her home to Sunbury. It was around eight miles and the walk took us a couple of hours, so we had a good chat. I asked her whether she would like to go to the pictures with me, she said yes, and that was how we started out together.

A year later, on a Thursday, the date being 12th July, 1956, we were married at Ealing Registry Office. It was a small affair, typical of the time. Nell had given birth to a third daughter, Josephine, and they came along with my other two half-sisters, Maureen and Chris, but Dad was working and couldn't get the time off. Di's younger sister, Joan, and a few other relatives and friends were there.

Joan was four years younger than Di, but they were very close.

Their childhood had not been a happy one – as very young girls, with their father serving in Egypt, their mother had eloped with another man, leaving them to be passed around relatives until they were re-united with their father a few years later. Their mother inflicted many scars on them, the consolation being that the experiences bonded Di and Joan in a closeness that has endured their entire lives.

I wasn't permitted to have anybody to stay with me at my digs, so we began our married life together living in one room at Dad and Nell's house. Di became pregnant with our first son, Stephen, who was born in November 1957. I had to find somewhere for us to live, and I was told about a man who owned a large house in Hanworth Road, Hampton, and who let out rooms. We arranged to meet him at his café at The Mount, Hanworth, on an evening after I had finished work. He was busy serving customers, so we took a seat to wait for him. His radio was playing music when the programme was interrupted to announce the news of the Munich air crash[51]. All the customers seemed very upset.

The house was in a poor state, and the accommodation he had for us was a single large room on the ground floor, with a stone sink in a corner. We felt we had little choice but to take it, and at least it wasn't too far for me to get to work. The garden was overgrown and the owners kept geese which chased Di when she went outside to hang the washing. She wasn't too keen on that, and I knew this could only be a short-term option, so I decided that I needed to start saving money to find somewhere better to live, perhaps get a mortgage. I stopped smoking and took an evening/weekend job helping to tend the glorious garden and greenhouse next door that belonged to a councillor, Cllr Crane. He sold the produce he grew, although my role was basically to shovel manure.

Six months later, we moved again, taking two rooms on the first floor of a house in Camden Avenue, Feltham, owned by Mr and Mrs Gates. They let us use the toilet but not the bathroom so we had to walk to the public baths in Feltham High Street for a bath. We weren't permitted to use the garden, but, fortunately, next door lived Mrs Darlow, who got friendly with Di, and she was happy to let us visit her garden. She also arranged for our clothes washing to be done by a 'bag wash' service that collected the dirty clothing and returned them damp but clean.

Stephen was coming up to a year old when Di fell pregnant for a second time. In the first few days of 1959, when she was around eighteen weeks pregnant, she complained of a severe pain in her stomach. She went to our GP, Dr Chandler, in Hanworth Road, Feltham, who told her that he thought that the baby had died. He gave her an injection and sent her home. I got home from work and sat with Di until she gave birth at four o'clock in the morning. The baby looked perfect but had been too small to survive.

We had no phone nor means to contact anyone, so I waited a few hours and went to a phone box to call Dr Chandler, who came out in mid-morning to examine Di and the baby. I was told to do the worst thing I'd ever been asked – to wrap the small corpse with the afterbirth and cremate it in our kitchen fire. It was heart-breaking.

Every penny counted for us, so I couldn't contemplate taking any time off from my job, and I went into work as normal the following day. Fortunately, Joan was a great help and comfort for Di. Joan had met a chap, Derek Brown, who she married later that year. Derek has since become almost a brother to me, although a later conversation revealed that our paths had crossed previously, unbeknown to either of us. I told Derek that I had lived in Roseville Avenue, and he said that he had dated a girl, Josie, who had lived in that road, and that one Christmas he'd slept in the lodger's bedroom while the lodger was away. Josie was the name of my landlord's youngest daughter, and further discussion revealed that, while I was staying over at Di's mum's house in Sunbury, Derek was in my bed in Hounslow.

JAMES PITTS

CHAPTER EIGHTEEN

Towards the end of 1959, Di fell pregnant again, with the baby due in August of the following year. We tried to put our names on the local authority's waiting list for a council house, but we were told that it was closed. We couldn't continue to live where we were, and I decided that we had to look for a place to buy.

Di went to an estate agents and was told about a house in Longford Avenue, Bedfont, around a mile to the other side of Feltham. It was a 1930s, two-bedroom, end-of-terrace house that was on the market for the price of two thousand five hundred pounds.[52]

It was unheard of to get a one-hundred percent mortgage, so I had to find a way to raise the deposit, which was five hundred pounds. A few years previously, I had been given a gold watch from Sperry's for fifteen years' service (before and after the war) and in all this time I had been paying into the firm's pension policy.

The company had a scheme whereby employees could take the money from their pension pot as a lump sum and carry on working for them thereafter, and I had enough money saved to fund the deposit.

I applied for the money, but, while this was going through, the rules were changed and the only way I could get the money was to leave the firm. We were committed to the house, so I felt that I had little choice.

The house had been advertised at two thousand five hundred pounds 'or near offer'. We asked about putting in a lower bid, but the estate agent told us that so many people were interested in the property that we might lose it to someone who would offer the full amount.

We got a mortgage for two thousand pounds. Interest rates were about four per cent and our repayments worked out to be around thirteen pounds a month. I got a new job in Chiswick on a weekly wage of some fifteen pounds – I don't think nowadays you could get a mortgage anywhere near London with monthly repayments that are the equivalent of a working man's weekly wage.

We had to wait to complete the purchase because our vendors were trying to buy a boarding house in Brighton and there was a hitch. Our building society said that it wasn't prepared to give us all the money we needed because the house was in a bit of a mess and needed some work to bring it up to scratch. They said they would withhold one hundred pounds, which could have caused the purchase to fall through because I was stretched to the limit.

Our second son, Mark, was born in August while we were still living at Mr and Mrs Gates. They wanted my growing family out of their home, and we were desperate to move, so I committed myself to doing the work required to bring our new home up to scratch. Each evening after I had finished work, I went straight to the house, with my father-in-law, Benny, sometimes joining me to help. The property was filthy. I had to modernise and redecorate the bathroom, and there was about an inch of dirt and dust on top of the toilet cistern, which was high up on the wall. As I was cleaning it, the woman brought me a sandwich, which was very kind of her. I thanked her, but, after she returned downstairs I tipped it down the toilet and flushed it away. I couldn't bring myself to eat it among the filth of the bathroom.

Her husband had served in the Army and had obtained some green paint which had been used to camouflage tanks and other military hardware. He had coated several of the walls of the house with it, and it proved impossible to get off – we tried several ways of removing it without success. We decided to wallpaper over the top of it, and there were evenings when we were papering the walls of these people's living room as they were sat in their chairs watching television.

The ceilings had been covered in whitewash which had been mixed out of paste and water. We tried to paint over the top of it but it flaked off, then we tried to put wallpaper on it, but that wouldn't stick. I had to rub the whole lot off, and that was hard work.

We took possession of the house in the autumn of 1960, and there was still plenty of work to do. The previous owners had left a rocking chair behind in an upstairs bedroom, and, when I went to throw it out, I discovered that it was covered in woodworm. I lifted up the lino, and the floorboards were also full of woodworm. It was a similar story in the bathroom, where several of the floorboards were in a rotten state. I had to replace these and treat others.

I didn't have a lot of spare time because I had taken a job with a small engineering firm under the arches at Chiswick Park Underground Station. That was around eight miles from home, but, with the A4 flyover at Chiswick being extended, the extensive roadworks caused my journey to take up to ninety minutes in each direction. Mind you, at least I had a job. Six months after I left Sperry's, they closed the factory at Feltham and moved to

Bracknell. A few years later, that folded, and they gave up in Britain to become based entirely in the States.

Our third son, Christopher, was born in July 1963, and, with this and the frustration of such a lengthy drive to work, I looked for a job closer to home. I got taken on by Timex at their factory on the North Feltham Trading Estate, which was only a handy ten-minute walk from home. I was employed making gyroscopes for the Polaris missile in the States.

Living next door to us was an Irish family, Larry and Carmel Breen, who had come over to London for work a few years previously. They had a daughter and twin sons who were a year or so older than Steve. In 1965, they moved back to Tramore, near Waterford on the south coast of Ireland, and we went to visit them the following year, travelling by train and boat. It was there that we watched on television as England won the World Cup final 4-2 against West Germany.

Two years later, we went on holiday with Joan and Derek, who by now had four children – daughters Maxine, Sharon and Tracey and a son, Tony. We went with them on a camping holiday to Paignton, although the journey from London to Devon was not very enjoyable because the Exeter by-pass had not yet been built. It took us around twelve hours to cover a distance of two hundred miles. The weather was kind and we spent a lot of time on the beach, with the kids in and out of the sea.

One afternoon, Chris complained that his leg was hurting, so Joan took Tony out of his pushchair to let Chris sit down. He fell asleep immediately and, as I looked at him, I saw red streaks from his groin to his knee. I took a closer look and saw what looked like a puncture mark on his knee.

We took him to a local doctor, who seemed to think that Chris had been bitten by something in the sea, causing an infection to set in. He said the condition was so serious that, in the days before antibiotics (which I could remember but Di couldn't), his leg would have required amputation. The doctor prescribed drugs and they gradually did the trick. Chris was not allowed to walk on that leg for the rest of his holiday, so he had to lay on a sun bed and watch the other children playing together, which wasn't so nice for a young lad!

JAMES PITTS

CHAPTER NINETEEN

We stayed in touch with our former neighbours, the Breens, and we returned to Ireland for another visit in 1969. This time, we decided to travel by car, so I told Di to buy as much tinned and packaged food as she could because we could take that with us. Di went a little bit overboard, and, by the time we came to leave, I had to squeeze into my Vauxhall Victor estate a big pile of food along with a tent, all our luggage, two adults and three young boys!

This was in the days before seatbelts, so I moulded makeshift seats among the baggage for Mark and Chris, while Steve sat with me and Di on a bench seat in the front.

The simplest sea crossing for us would have been the ferry from Fishguard on the Welsh coast to Rosslare in the south-east of Ireland. However, this was fully booked for when we wished to travel, so we decided to drive to Scotland to take a ferry from Stranraer to Larne in Northern Ireland. After a long drive and an overnight stop near Dumfries to sleep in the car, we arrived at the port to find a lengthy queue of vehicles whose drivers had obviously had the same idea.

I joined the line of vehicles in the hope of getting a crossing that day, but by evening, with the last ferry due to depart, we had resigned ourselves to missing out and spending another night dozing in the car. However, ten minutes before departure, our name was called out and I was told to drive on board – we were the last vehicle to get on a ferry that day.

On our arrival in Larne, it was getting on towards midnight. It was dark and I didn't have a map, so I decided to follow the signs to Belfast and continue south on the A1 heading towards the Republic of Ireland. There had been quite a lot of sectarian trouble in Northern Ireland that summer and Di was a little apprehensive about going anywhere near Belfast, but I told her that we'd pass through the city before anybody was awake, although we did see a lot of young men loitering on street corners.

After clearing Belfast, we drove through a couple of towns without incident, but, as we were driving through Newry, the car started to play up. Again, there was a fair number of people hanging about on the streets, but the car was making such a noise that I had no choice but to stop it and get out to take a look at the engine. I saw that the crankshaft had become loose, so I crawled underneath the car, aware that I was being watched by a growing crowd of youths. I was able to tighten it and we made our getaway without incident.

I was surprised to see no guards at the border, and the journey thereafter was uneventful until we were close to Waterford and a large seagull flew into our windscreen to give us all a bit of a scare. It was six-thirty in the morning, and we were all ready for a long sleep.

We stayed with the Breens for three weeks, and, on the last weekend of our holiday, I went camping with Larry in the beautiful countryside close to the sea cliffs. I took Steve and Mark, while Larry brought his three children, Susan, Paul and Raymond, and we arranged for Carmel and Dianne to prepare lunch for the following day, a Sunday, and come with Chris to meet us. During the Saturday night, Steve complained of a headache and vomited several times, so we took him back to the Breen's house, where we put him to bed. However, his head was causing him so much pain that he took to banging it against a wall. Carmel called out a doctor, who said he suspected that my son had meningitis, and he told us to take him immediately to Ardkeen Hospital in Waterford. On arrival there, he was given a lumbar puncture[53] and diagnosed with viral meningitis,[54] although the doctors did their best to assure us that he should make a full recovery.

We were told that he would be kept in hospital for about a week and that he would not be able to travel home in the car. Because I had been led to understand that Ireland had a reciprocal health agreement with the United Kingdom, we hadn't taken out any insurance cover to pay for hospital fees. However, I had been misinformed, which meant that we had to find a way to pay the bill, which was going to be the equivalent to several weeks' wages for me. The only realistic solution was for us to leave Steve in the care of our friends and return home so that I could do some overtime and Di could find temporary work to cover the cost of the hospital and to pay for Steve's flight home. The doctors felt that he would be fit enough to travel back around a fortnight after leaving hospital, and Larry said that he would drive Steve to Dublin and put him on a flight to London.

While we were staying with the Breens, what became known as 'The Troubles'[55] ignited throughout Northern Ireland, with many homes burnt down and lots of violence between the different communities. It was clearly not the best idea to attempt to drive through the province in a car carrying a British number plate, so we drove to Rosslare and managed to get on a ferry crossing to Fishguard. It was a difficult moment leaving the country without our eldest son, and I had to comfort Di as she stood on the ferry deck looking back until she could no longer see the Irish coastline.

It was dark when we disembarked, and I needed to find a garage to put some petrol in the car. By the time I had done that, all the London-bound traffic had departed and I had little idea which direction to follow (I still hadn't got around to buying a map!). I saw a sign which said 'Newport' so I took that road on the assumption that it was going to take us to Haverfordwest and onto the A40 and A48 towards Newport, Gwent. I drove through twisting roads into the Pembrokeshire Coast National Park, over steep hills and into valleys, thinking that this seemed a bit unusual for a major route but, still, the signs pointed to Newport and so I continued. The car's headlights even picked out rats running across the bumpy road. We eventually arrived at 'Newport' which, as you have probably worked out for yourself, was not the one that we wanted.[56] Rather than being the last Welsh city on the way to England, this was a small town of around one thousand people. We arrived there in the middle of the night, so I pulled the car up at the side of the road and got a couple of hours' sleep before we set off on our long journey home.

We arrived home late on a Saturday afternoon, and, on the following Tuesday, Di returned to work with an agency for which she had worked part-time when the boys were at school. Jean Scurry, who with her husband Ray had bought the house from the Breens, agreed to look after Mark and Chris and, on the Wednesday, she took them, together with her own two small boys, to a sports day which had been organised by a local church group at Bedfont recreation ground. Mark was wearing a new Chelsea kit and trainers, presents for his ninth birthday a couple of weeks previously.

Di had only been home from work a short while when a friend, Avis, who lived in the same road, knocked on the door to tell her that Mark had been struck by a car. Leaving Avis to ring me at work, Di ran across the recreation ground to Hatton Road, where a church helper told her that Mark had been severely injured and that he had been taken in an ambulance to Ashford

Hospital. Di was given a lift to the hospital, where she went into the accident and emergency department to hear Mark crying out for her. The nurses blocked her way, and took her into a 'small room to wait for me.

I was in a bit of a state by the time I arrived, and I walked along the unit's main corridor pulling open the cubicle curtains as I tried to find Mark. I only stopped when a nurse took me by the arm and led me to where Di was waiting.

Eventually, a surgeon and a doctor came to speak to us. They said that Mark had numerous injuries, including a broken femur, a broken jaw, a severe cut to the back of his head (and they suspected a fractured skull), puncture wounds to his legs, many cuts and bruises, while his ear had been almost sliced off by what they believed was the car's wing-mirror. The head injury was of particular concern, and they warned us that his injuries were life-threatening.

He had been taken into the intensive care unit, and the doctors took us to see him. As I looked into his room and saw his small body covered in blood-stained dressings and with drips seemingly everywhere, I was struck by an overwhelming sense of helplessness. It was the worst feeling of my life, and I would have readily traded my life for that of my son.

Mark was too poorly for them to operate on him that evening, but they said that they would monitor him throughout the night and, if possible, commence surgery the following day. We asked for one of us to be allowed to stay at the hospital with him, but we were told to go home and return the following morning. Because we still needed to raise the money to get Steve home and because I would not be paid for taking any time off work, we decided that Di would go to the hospital while I would go to the factory and work my normal hours, and then meet her there afterwards.

On her arrival the next day, Mark was still heavily sedated, but

Di was told that his condition had improved enough for the surgeons to carry out an operation on his broken leg later that afternoon. The nurse handed her the remains of the Chelsea kit and trainers that had been cut off him the previous day, and Di stood in the corridor and sobbed her heart out. Joan had arrived at the hospital ahead of me, and I turned up to find them both crying over the clothing.

Mark was taken to theatre and his broken leg was successfully set, but they decided that they had to wait to operate on his jaw. A surgeon from Mount Vernon hospital in Slough came a few days later to carry out that procedure.

The head injury had been the major concern because it appeared that the collision with the car, which the police told us had been speeding at probably twice the speed limit for the small village road, had caused the back of Mark's head to strike the kerb. The surgeons at the hospital were fantastic, and were able to report that Mark had not suffered any brain damage and that they were hopeful that, in time, he would make a full recovery.

We were able to get Steve back from Ireland. I collected him at the airport, but I didn't tell him anything about Mark. When we arrived home, he asked where his brother was, and we had to inform him about the accident.

Mark was to remain in hospital for a further three months. He returned to school in the new year and gradually got back to his normal self.

There have been times since that summer when life has not always been as I'd want it to be, but in those moments I tell myself that, like my own father, I could have lost two sons in tragic circumstances. I'm grateful that they have both been able to grow into the men, fathers (and grandfather!) that they now are.

CHAPTER TWENTY

I left Timex in 1970 when the company lost its Polaris contract and laid off a lot of its workers. Shortly before I finished, a young lad came into work one morning and asked for an afternoon off because he needed to go into London to record a performance for the television programme 'Top of the Pops'. His name was Ray Dorset and his band was Mungo Jerry — the song was 'In The Summertime',[57] which you can hear on the radio even now. He had been living in Bedfont when he wrote the song.

I took a job as machine shop supervisor with Data Recording in Staines, a company which later became Newbury Data. It made industrial printers, enormous things.

After our experiences of the previous summer, I told Di that, for our next holiday, I wanted to find somewhere not too far from home where we could park the car and rest up. With Joan and Derek and their children, we went to a small holiday camp, Gibson's, in Bracklesham Bay, Sussex. Di's mother and stepfather joined us, and we had a good time, even if the basic wooden shacks that provided our accommodation brought back memories of my wartime billetings! We went to the bar each evening, leaving the kids asleep in the chalet with a handkerchief tied to the door handle. The camp employed staff to patrol the grounds and, when they heard a child calling out, they came into the bar to announce, 'Baby crying in chalet number XX.' Imagine doing that now!

We went back the following year for Whitsun week, when we were joined by Jean and Ray and their boys. We had another nice time so we returned for a further week in August, when Di's father and step-mother also came long. Holidaying here became an annual event for all our families during each Whitsun week, with more and more friends and family members joining us – we grew in numbers to some thirty-five in total before it all came to an end. The journey from our home near Heathrow Airport was only some sixty-five miles, but we stopped at several pubs on the way to arrive just in time for the annual England v Scotland football match that provided the climax to the now defunct Home International Championship.[58] We had several fantastic holidays there, with the likes of the still 'unknown' Michael Barrymore and Roger de Courcey[59] among the entertainers who kept us amused. Both were to become big television personalities over the following years – Roger was part of a unique ventriloquist act with 'Nookie Bear'.

One of the families who came with us went by the name of Evans, and they lived in Porthcawl, a holiday resort in south Wales. In August 1975, we were staying at their home when we heard on the radio a news report about a holiday camp at Bracklesham Bay being destroyed by fire. It was Gibson's. We had made reservations for a reunion weekend the following month, but that was cancelled and the camp never re-opened as Gibson's. We tried other holiday camps but never managed to replicate the atmosphere we had so enjoyed.

Around this time I joined a local Royal Naval Association club for no other reason than it gave me a cheap place to drink. They organised a short break to Jersey, and Di and I signed up for it, with Joan and Derek deciding to join us. I had understood it to be a coach journey with ferry crossing from Southampton, but, when we arrived on the south coast, I was a bit shocked to be informed that we would be flying on a small aircraft, a Britten-Norman Islander.[60]

Having survived three plane crashes during the war, as well as enduring some other unpleasant experiences towards the end of my time in the Fleet Air Arm, I had quietly decided never to fly again. However, I felt I couldn't spoil everybody's holiday, so I took to the skies for the first time in over thirty years. The flight was fine, and it paved the way for further flights over the next thirty years to destinations that have included Malta, Portugal, Spain, France, Italy, Greece, Corfu, Russia and the Czech Republic.

I had been working for Data Recording for seventeen years when I went to an exhibition in Birmingham. I took a company car from the company garage, and I returned it late the same evening. 'What are you doing here, Jim?' the garage supervisor asked as I handed him the keys. 'Haven't you heard, your place was shut down today and everybody was sent home.' I saw some lights on in the office, and I spoke to a chap in personnel, who said, 'Oh, we were going to send you a letter.' I thought that was nice of them.

I was sixty-three years of age, and I didn't think that I'd get another job. I rang around some firms and got taken on by Timex again, in another of their divisions in Feltham, and I stayed there until I was sixty-five.

'It's time to retire, Jim,' I told myself — but other people had other ideas!

Di arranged a surprise retirement party for me at Hounslow Football Club in Denbigh Road, Hounslow,[61] where I had taken my sons as young lads to watch their first football match and where the three of them played together some years later. She invited lots of people I had worked with over the years. It was nice to catch up with some of those that I hadn't seen in a long time, and one of them, Harvey, asked me what I was going to do next. I told him I didn't have any idea, and he gave me his card and said for me to give him a call. He had set up a company that repaired printer heads.

I phoned him and he asked me to pop along to see him, with the result that I worked for him for the next ten years – initially part-time and then full-time. His company packed up in 1999, when I was seventy-five, and I finally got to retire.

My family had grown during this time. Steve got married, had three children, got divorced and got married again – I found his separation and divorce quite hard, I guess because I'd come from a generation that had felt it necessary to stick together. But this was a different generation, and several of my nieces also got divorced. Mark married and had three children and then he, too, separated, while Chris seemed to settle for the single life. Britain had changed tremendously since the war, and younger people don't seem to have the patience to stick at things the way we did, although that may well be simply because we'd had less choice. We bought our home in 1960 and were still living in it in 2015. When the Breens moved back to Ireland, the house was bought by the Scurrys, who were still living in it in 2015. On the other side of us was a couple, Jean and Sam Chant, who had bought their house five years before us and stayed in it for nearly sixty years until they died a few months apart in 2013. They had two daughters.

Three houses, side by side, with a total of over one hundred and sixty years of the same families occupying them – how often is that going to happen again?

Sam, who died at the age of ninety-three, had also served during the war, but not once did we speak about it. After his death, his daughters asked Di to help sort out his paperwork, and she discovered that he had fought Rommel in the North African desert and that he'd had shrapnel in his back which they could not remove. It was enough of a problem that he got a disability pension right up to the day he died.

JAMES PITTS

CHAPTER TWENTY-ONE

Over the past couple of decades, I have become increasingly comfortable about talking about the war – some people might say too comfortable! Everything changed for me on the day I went to Hyde Park in 1995 for the commemorations to mark the fiftieth anniversary of the end of the conflict in Europe.

Di and the boys said that they had made arrangements to attend, and they got on at me about it. I said that I didn't want to go, but they kept on and I relented. They had a leaflet that said ex-servicemen could wear their medals, and they asked me about mine. I told them that they were in a box in the loft, where they had been since we had lived in the house. They made me go up and retrieve the box, which is the first time that they had seen it.

The boys told me to put the medals on but I didn't want to do that – the war seemed such a long time ago. They told me to put them in my pocket so that, should I get there and see everybody else wearing theirs, I could put mine on. That is what I did.

At Hyde Park, there were a few pole marquees marked up

for the different branches of the forces, and in one I met a couple of air-gunners who had been on HMS Premier with me. We had a good drink-up, exchanged contact details and said that we should keep in touch, although we had scattered all over the country.

Three years later, one of the air-gunners got in touch to say that they had a club, the Telegraphist Air-Gunners Association, which met regularly at the Union Jack Club near Waterloo railway station in London. He asked me to go along for a meeting, which I did and which I enjoyed. I was fully retired and had some spare time, so I joined the association.

At one meeting, I sat next to Dennis Lyddel, an air-gunner who had also trained in Canada and who had been sent to Yarmouth around three months ahead of me. I got on well with him and we reminisced about our experiences. Dennis told me that he had regularly visited a café in the area, and that he had got engaged to a girl who worked there. To my astonishment, he told me her name – Della Doucette, the girl to whom I had also got engaged! And such a short while after Dennis had left Canada to return to Britain! We laughed about it, although neither of us had any idea whether she ever got around to marrying an air-gunner.

Around the same time, George Chapman, who lived in a flat beneath Chris in Chiswick, west London, and who had served in the Navy, took me along to the Russian Convoy Club, which met in Kennington, London. I joined this club, and I have been attending ever since. I hadn't served with any of the men I have met there, although two had been on HMS Cotton and had been on the same convoy as I had, while another chap, who was in the Navy, had been in the same convoy, manning the guns on a Merchant Navy ship.

The numbers have dwindled – when I joined, we had an average of thirty members attending our meetings, but death and the inability to continue to travel meant that a decade later there were only eight or nine of us. Nobody can live forever, and it won't be too long until this club folds. I was only a week past my eighteenth birthday when I got my papers, so there aren't too many air crew who could be younger than me, although you could join the Navy at seventeen and the Merchant Navy at sixteen, and that's where some of our more younger members come from.

I had my first encounter with royalty in 2000 when I attended the unveiling of a memorial to those who had been lost while serving with the Fleet Air Arm and the Royal Navy Air Service.[62] The memorial is on the Embankment alongside the River Thames in London, opposite the London Eye, and it is dedicated to those who lost their lives in both world wars, as well as more recent conflicts such as the Falklands and the first Gulf War.

With Di, I had been invited to attend the event by the Telegraphist Air-Gunners Association. As we sat waiting for the unveiling to be carried out by the Prince of Wales, a chap came over to me and said, 'Jimmy Pitts, how are you?' It was an air-gunner from 856 Squadron who I hadn't seen for fifty-odd years. His name was Ray Law and he went by the nickname 'Jungle' after the wartime film 'Jungle Law'. He said to me, 'I remember you as the best looking bloke in our squadron...what happened?' Di laughed her head off at that.

After the unveiling, Di and I paid thirty pounds each to be entered into a draw, with a number of people having their name selected for a tour of St James's Palace followed by a reception there. We were among those chosen and we were lined up to be presented to Prince Charles. He chatted to us and something was said about Great Ormond Street Hospital. Di told him that we'd had a bit of experience with that hospital because two of our grandchildren, Mark's boys Christian and Glenn, had been in and out of it since birth. He spoke to us about them for some while and seemed very concerned, and he wished them well. I was quite impressed with the way in which he spoke to us and the compassion that he showed.

Unfortunately, we weren't allowed to take our cameras into the palace with us, although I was later given some photographs by a naval photographer who obviously had permission to take some pictures.

CHAPTER TWENTY-TWO

In the summer of 2004, Chris paid for Di and I to fly to Norway and stay at a lovely hotel in the village of Balestrand on the shore of the Sognefjord, which is the largest fjord in the country and the third longest in the world. From our room, we had a view over the deep blue fjord to the amazing Gualarfjellet mountains, and it would be difficult to think of a more spectacular sight.

This holiday brought back so many memories for me, and, as I stood by the side of the water, I vividly recalled how, nearly sixty years previously (which seemed no time at all), our aircrews had flown wing-tip to wing-tip just one hundred and fifty feet above the water to drop our mines and scarper with the German guns firing at us from the banks.

As I reflected, I thought that this experience, in so many ways, had been more frightening for me than the convoys. We had been instructed to fly in strict formation, which meant we could not take evasive action, and should our plane have been clipped by another, we would have been sent into the freezing water with no hope of rescue.

The mine-laying runs to the fjords had been my first

experience of combative warfare, and it was those memories that came flooding back as I stood on the banks of the Sognefjord.

With Di holding onto my arm beside me, I said to her that it was, thankfully, a very different world to how it had been in those wartime years. I shuddered at the thought of what had happened to some of our chaps and what could have happened to me. We had been well trained, but we were no more than boys and nothing could have prepared me for the alarm I had felt when we had flown over the water with bullets hurtling towards us and flak exploding in the skies around us.

Many of us veterans had long felt that those who had served on the Arctic Convoys deserved recognition distinct from the Atlantic Star[63] that we had been awarded at the end of the war.

The Russian Convoy Club asked Commander Eddie Grenfell,[64] who had survived the bombing and sinking of HMS Empire Lawrence in 1942, and who was four years older than me, to lead a campaign to get the convoy veterans our own Arctic Star medal.

There was absolutely nothing wrong with the Atlantic Star, but I think most people would agree that the convoys through the Arctic waters took place in a completely separate theatre to the Atlantic. I'm taking nothing away from those who saw service in the Atlantic, where the German U-boats were a constant threat and so many men were lost, but the concentration of enemy submarines and war planes, combined with the appalling weather, made the Arctic Convoys quite unique. Even Winston Churchill used the words 'the worst journey in the world' to describe them.

Cdr Grenfell was the perfect man for the task. His daughter, Trudie, later described him as an 'unstoppable force' and I think that summed him up better than anything I could say. By all accounts, he spent up to eighteen hours a day writing letters to politicians, civil servants, forces personnel and anybody he felt could help our campaign. His passion for our cause was fantastic, and, although he faced many setbacks, he never let these dissuade him.

Our branch of the air-gunners association followed his lead, and we received quite a lot of support from Members of Parliament, other politicians and dignitaries, and those in the services who had recognised that we should not have been grouped together with the Atlantic campaign. They seemed to be quite taken by our claim and everybody seemed to be aware of the words that Churchill had used to describe the convoys.

However, we didn't seem to get very far, and the Government and bureaucrats tended to bat back our requests by saying that the convoys had been recognised with the award of the Atlantic Star. They also said that it was too long after the war for them to start issuing a new medal.

We continued to write letters to people who we thought might be interested in hearing our side of things, but we weren't too pushy and nothing much seemed to happen other than a lot of people wrote back to agree with us.

In early 2005, we were invited to a reception for convoy veterans at Ten Downing Street, home of the Prime Minister. There was a couple of hundred of us there, as well as plenty of people from the Admiralty. The room was packed, the wine flowed and I got quite hot so I sat down for a few minutes on a sofa where I had the First Sea Lord, Sir Alan West, on one side of me and lord somebody or other on the other side. I was in fine company!

I got up to fill my glass and I wandered over to where a few of the chaps from our association were standing. We were having a bit of a laugh when Tony Blair came into the room. He walked straight over to where I was standing, so we started on at him about giving us the campaign medal. The room was so crowded that the poor man was unable to get away from us as we badgered him, and he said that he would personally look into the matter, although he did say that he couldn't give any guarantees. His minders finally made their way through the crowd to take him away, and I think he was quite relieved to escape us.

The next day, it was announced that we would be awarded an emblem[65] rather than a medal, which caused quite a lot of upset among some of the chaps. Cdr Grenfell was very unhappy, and when he was interviewed by the BBC he described the decision as 'dreadful' and vowed to continue his campaign.[66]

Considering the attitude of the officials we had encountered, I'd had little hope of getting a medal, and I thought that, at least, an emblem was some sort of recognition. It was something we could wear in the lapel of our blazers, and we were told that we would be allowed to put it in with our medals.

I was grateful that the Prime Minister had listened to us and, to an extent, acted on our wishes, which was reasonable of him. More has come out about him since he left office and people don't see him in the same way now, but at least he had invited us to Downing Street and taken on board our argument.

Within our association, we decided to accept the emblem but to continue with our campaign for the medal, and there was going to be no stopping Cdr Grenfell in his campaign for a medal. The local newspaper in Portsmouth printed some posters with slogans like, 'The Arctic Convoy Veterans Demand Justice' and 'Veterans Deserve a Medal' and Cdr Grenfell and the Portsmouth News organised a march for them to show these off.

CHAPTER TWENTY-THREE

The year 2005 marked the sixtieth anniversary of the end of the war, and I was given the opportunity to return to Russia for the first time since our convoy set off from Murmansk for home all those years ago in 1945.

It wasn't something that I had ever expected to do, or I had even thought too deeply about. The opportunity arose because the people running the National Lottery, Camelot, supported a scheme called 'Heroes Return' by handing out grants to assist veterans' organisations and individuals to return to a place where they had served during the war. Our club decided that it would be fitting to go to Russia. Some of the chaps had previously made their own private trips to Murmansk and had recommended it.

Gordon Long, secretary of the Russian Convoy Club, worked with a travel agency to put together an itinerary that would see us stay for five days each in Murmansk and Arkhangelsk, and stop off in St Petersburg on the way home.

The grant from Camelot covered the cost of the trip for both me and Di, who was put down to go as my 'carer', although she made the trip on crutches, having undergone a knee replacement operation only a few weeks before we departed. We were scheduled to fly from London Gatwick to St Petersburg before transferring to another airport in the Russian city for an internal flight to Murmansk. Mark drove us to Gatwick, where Gordon had said that he would give us our flight tickets. There were around forty veterans in our party plus wives, carers and a few officials, and he doled out all the tickets, although he didn't seem to have any for me and Di, plus another lady. He was fumbling around, in a bit of a panic, when, from his pocket, he took out some tickets in the names of people who had withdrawn from the trip. He said to me, 'Don't worry, I've got some spare ones,' and with that he crossed out the names on the tickets and wrote our names in black ink on three of them. I said to him, 'They won't accept that,' but he said they would.

We went to the check-in desk, and the first thing the woman said was, 'Who's done this to the tickets?' I worried that we would not be allowed onto the plane, but one of the top executives from Aeroflot had come to see us off and, when he heard what was happening, he stepped in and got the check-in people to issue tickets in our names.

By the time this had been sorted, all the others had walked off to go through security. Di had to take everything slowly because she was on crutches, so this chap organised a buggy to give us a ride out to the plane. We arrived at it before the others!

In total, there was around one hundred of us on that plane, while another plane took approximately one hundred and fifty people from the North Russia Club. That meant about two hundred and fifty of us arrived in St Petersburg, and the Russians handled that number without any difficulty other than a few people getting the wrong dinner!

The North Russia Club had a slightly different schedule to ours, and we went our separate ways. We flew up to Murmansk, which had changed beyond all recognition from when I had last seen it – it was terrific to see how prosperous it seemed to be, and how happy the people were, compared to the stark poverty we had witnessed in 1945.

We were taken by bus to a lovely hotel in the city, which was our base for the next five days.

Over the years, I hadn't thought too much about what the Russian people had been told about our convoys. If anything, I suspected that the former communist regime would have downplayed their role to fit in with the political climate of the Cold War.

So I was taken aback by the warmth of the reception we received from everybody each time we ventured out of the hotel. We got a taste of what it must have been like to be the Beatles! As soon as anybody spotted us, they came up to us to shake our hand, to give us a kiss and to have their photograph taken with us. It was truly humbling how well informed all the people, old and young, were about the convoys and how grateful they were for them. Through a translator, one Russian man kissed me on both cheeks and told me that he would never forget the sacrifices that the convoys had made to help his people. It was quite touching.

9th May is known as Victory Day[67] in Russia, and this particular one marked the sixtieth anniversary of the end of the war in Europe. It was a huge occasion for the people of the city, virtually all of whom seemed to be out on the streets, and they were keen for us to play a prominent role in their commemorations.

HMS Sutherland, the most powerful frigate in the British fleet, came into port to further represent Great Britain. The Duke of York and the First Sea Lord, Sir Alan West, were also there.

To honour the Arctic Convoys, Murmansk has a statue on a hill outside the city centre. We were asked to lead a march up to it, which we were honoured to do, and there we took part in a ceremony there to remember all those who had died.

At the conclusion of the formalities, the organisers released hundreds of red balloons into the sky in memory of the lost. It was quite a sight, especially as the skies were a deep blue colour. The day before it had snowed quite heavily, but this day was a beautiful cloud-free one.

We went back to the main square, which was full of stalls and packed with people, who came at us from right, left and centre to give us drinks and shake our hand. The atmosphere was uplifting.

Everybody seemed to want to talk to us, to say thank-you for the convoys, and I was very impressed at their English language abilities. I had a good drink that day, and I wasn't the only veteran to do that!

We were invited to a function on the Sutherland which was to be attended by Prince Andrew and Sir Alan West. We were told that we were to be introduced to them, so we were organised into a circle. Standing next to me was our standard bearer who, each time he carried the standard at a ceremony, received a badge to mark the occasion. He had dozens of them fixed down one side of his blazer. I didn't know him too well because he wasn't a member of our club, he came from one of the branches elsewhere in the country, but I could see that he was proud to be doing his job. When Prince Andrew got to him, he looked at his jacket and said to him, 'Where did you get all those – out of a Cornflakes' packet?' I don't think that the Duke was in any way trying to be offensive, it was just a silly comment, but the standard bearer got very upset and looked like he was about to cry. He said afterwards that he hadn't found the remark the slightest bit funny and spoke about making a complaint, although I didn't see the need for that. Sometimes you just have to accept these things and laugh them off.

We were given a tour of the Sutherland and were shown all the modern weaponry. They had guns which could hit a target sixty miles away – a bit different to my day.

The Russian people couldn't do enough for us, and those five days in Murmansk were an absolute delight. We were guests of honour at receptions and dinners, and we were taken on a number of excursions, but what I enjoyed most was being taken to visit schools in the city, where the children all seemed to know so much about our wartime activities. Each school we visited had a room dedicated to the convoys, and the children there knew far more about us than most people do back in Britain. We spoke to them about our experiences and answered their questions.

I was informed that around one hundred and fifty thousand schools throughout Russia have such a 'convoy room', each of them containing information about the purpose of the convoys, the journey, the dangers and the people involved in them. When we went to Arkhangelsk for the next stage of our visit, I saw a photograph of myself as an air-gunner, standing alongside my pilot and observer.

We were given the full VIP treatment. We were taken to most functions by coach, sometimes as many as four of them in convoy, with an ambulance following just in case it was needed (although it wasn't). At every set of traffic lights or junction, the police stopped all other traffic to let us through.

At the hotel, there was a noticeboard that contained details of the trips and functions that the veterans had been invited to attend. Many of these had restrictions on the numbers of people able to attend, and each time Di and I went to the board we saw that all the places had been taken. We met a couple, Ted and Eve, who had been on similar trips before and who took us under their wing, and they said all you did was rub out the names of people who had put themselves down for more than one function and replace it with your own name. That's what we did, and we went to several lovely dinners with them. On each table, there was bottles of wine and vodka and, on a couple of occasions, we put the bottle of vodka into Di's bag to take back to the hotel. At one of the larger dinners, we were given naval collars to wear as we ate. At one function, I was presented with my Arctic emblem.

Our hotel had twelve floors. On the top floor was a bar that had panoramic views across land and water, which were all the more remarkable because even at midnight it was light outside. I went up there for a nightcap or two with some of the chaps, and a lot of the sailors from the Sutherland came in. They wanted to buy us drinks, and each night I sat drinking with them until one or two o'clock in the morning.

We flew to Arkhangelsk, where they also laid out the red carpet for us. We visited a naval academy that was made up of boys who had been orphaned and who were being prepared for a career in the Russian navy. They were aged fourteen to seventeen and they asked us questions about the war and our role in it. Sometimes the questions could be quite amusing. On one occasion, Di was sitting next to me with Ernie Kennedy the other side of her. One of the lads said to Ernie and Di, 'How long have you two been married?' Di joked, 'Oh, we're not married – we've just come away together!'

We flew back to St Petersburg for a few more days before our flight home. We were invited to the British and American consulates, as well as the Governor's mansion, which had once been a royal palace and which was very spectacular.

We had a terrific evening at the British consulate, where a reception was put on for us. One of the veterans had come over from Australia, and he got on the consulate's grand piano and played some of the old tunes. We had a great sing-song, with everybody in the room joining in.

This Aussie chap mentioned that it was his birthday the following day, so Di popped out of the hotel to get him a card. In the shop, she couldn't read the Russian language on the cards, so she picked out one which had a nice picture on it. We wrote on it and gave it to him. He asked one of the translators who accompanied us everywhere what the Russian words were, and he was told they said, 'Happy Birthday, Son'. Thereafter, he called Di 'Mum'.

Before setting off to Russia, we'd had no idea how much or how little Russian money we would need, so Di and I bought a few hundred pounds' worth of roubles from our local post office. With the red carpet being laid out for us everywhere we went, we spent less than we had anticipated.

Some of the others, however, ran short of roubles and they didn't have the time or the means to find somewhere to change their money. So, with our surplus money, Di took on a new role as a foreign exchange provider for our group, exchanging our roubles for English pounds. Some of the chaps started calling her Mrs Lloyd after the bank.

The day of our flight home came around quickly. I had really warmed to the Russian people, they couldn't have been nicer to us and they had seemed so interested in us. The ordinary people would share anything they had with you, and it was obvious how much even the younger generations valued the contribution we had made.

There had been the rare occasion during the intervening years when I had wondered whether they had appreciated our efforts and the huge cost of the convoys in terms of lives lost, but we all left there buoyed by their open display of gratitude and respect. It was terrible the suffering and starvation that the Russian people had gone through during the war years, but they clearly appreciated that even more of them would have been lost without the supplies that we had helped to deliver to them.

So, we set off for home, although our flight back to Gatwick was cancelled. We were bussed to an enormous hotel owned by Aeroflot and put up for the night before making the flight the following day.

While we had been in St Petersburg, there had been some talk that the Russian government wanted to present us with one of their top naval honours, the Medal of Ushakov.[68] This had been introduced towards the end of the war and was primarily for their sailors who had shown courage, but there was talk that they saw this medal as appropriate for us. However, the Russians could only present it to us with the permission of the British government, and it seemed that the bureaucrats in London had decided that this would be against the rules.

This was something we discussed at our next meeting, but there was little we could do about it other than continue to campaign for the Arctic Star. Some of the chaps felt that, should we be awarded that medal, it might help clear the way for us to receive the Medal of Ushakov.

CHAPTER TWENTY-FOUR

I was invited to attend my first Buckingham Palace garden party on 21st July, 2005, in the presence of the Princess Royal. I received my invitation through The Not Forgotten Association,[69] a marvellous organisation that works to support ex-servicemen in a variety of ways.

With Di, I had attended a few of their functions and social activities over the years, including a riverboat trip along the Thames and a couple of receptions in London. I wore my blazer with medals, while Di got herself dressed up.

Everybody was very nice to us, although we weren't presented to Princess Anne.

I must have behaved myself because I got invited back the following year, this time as part of the commemorations for a centenary of naval aviation. I knew that it was going to be a big affair because former and serving members of the Fleet Air Arm and Royal Naval Air Service had been invited, with their families, and it was said that more than five thousand people were expected to attend.

I had to go without Di, who had decided to stay home with

our pet Yorkshire Terrier Ben, who had been very poorly and was close to death. After our three sons had left home, we had taken to keeping Yorkies, our first one, Georgie, living until 1996, and Ben replacing her a few months later. Di didn't want to leave Ben at home alone, but, because this was an event for the Fleet Air Arm, I was keen to attend.

I went by train into London and went to the palace, but there were so many people there I couldn't find anybody I knew. I was sitting in a chair, alone, when I was approached by a chap who I had met previously because he was involved in the promotion of the Fleet Air Arm through things like designing stamps for use overseas.

He said that there was quite a group of other veterans in the gardens, and he took me over to them. I hadn't met any of them previously, but he introduced us to each other and we sat down around a table, where we had a nice drink and a chat.

One of them was an air-gunner who had been taken prisoner in the Far East after being shot down. He had been held for four years by the Japanese and suffered quite badly, including losing all his teeth, although he was grateful to have survived. As he spoke, I thought to myself that this could have been my fate because after the war in Europe had ended I had been put on standby to fly out to oppose the Japanese.

Di and I celebrated our golden wedding anniversary on 12th July, 2006. Our boys had often treated us to holidays and outings, and this time they took us away to some wooden lodges in the New Forest. We spent five lovely days there with them, Joan and Derek and most of our grandchildren.

Our eldest grandchild Lucy, who is Steve's eldest, was not with us because a couple of months previously she had set off to travel the world with her boyfriend, Matthew. A while later, they ended up in New Zealand and were so taken by it that they made it their home. They come back to England as often as they can, but Di finds the gaps quite difficult because she lives for her family. There were a few days in 2011 that were particularly worrying because Lucy and Matt were living in Christchurch when it was hit by a huge earthquake that destroyed much of the city. Because of the loss of power caused by the destruction, even the mobile phones weren't working and it was a long couple of days before we were told that they were both okay.

To mark our anniversary, our boys paid for Di and I to go on a Mediterranean cruise that summer aboard the Legend of the Seas. I recalled the only other occasion when I had been aboard a ship of such opulence – making my way across the Atlantic as a teenage boy who had seen nothing of the world.

Our air-gunners association decided to pack up. The numbers had been dwindling and it was difficult to keep it together because of our age and the geographical issues. Our members came from all over England, while we also had people living in Scotland, Ireland and Wales. We had no base of our own and used to meet now and then at the Union Jack Club at Waterloo, London. Even our treasurer lived in Scotland and had to fly down for the meetings, charging the flight to expenses.

I was on the committee, one of ten, while a further ten air-gunners made it to the meeting where it was proposed that we should fold. I felt that we should keep going for as long as we possibly could, but I was the only person to vote against closure and that was the end of that, although there was a bit of a hoo-ha over the money.

Our treasurer for many years had been Stuart Crawford, who had served in our squadron on the carrier, and who had reported that, at one time, we had £20,000 in the funds. After he died, somebody else took over the role, an associate member, and we had a few problems making contact with him. We didn't receive proper accounts, and, when we finally got them, they showed that there was only about £1,000 in the account. That was a bit of a shock. We had a vote on it, and gave half of that sum to the Not Forgotten Association and half to another organisation.

I was invited to a Buckingham Palace garden party for the third successive year on 8th July, 2010, this one again organised by The Not Forgotten Association and attended by the Duke of Gloucester. He seemed a pleasant enough man.

After my trip to Russia in 2005, I flew a couple more times to Spain to stay at a villa on the Costa Blanca owned by my niece Tracey and her husband Pat. Steve also paid for Di and I to visit the Czech Republic in the late autumn of 2009. His wife's family come from the ski resort of Špindlerův Mlýn, and this was the third time that we had been there to visit. I had even put on some skis and had a small go at downhill skiing when I had first gone there in 1996 – my first experience of skiing being at the age of seventy-one! At the time of the 2009 trip, I was 85 years of age, and I did say that that would probably be my last trip abroad.

I was proved wrong, however!

Although the air-gunners association packed in, our branch of the Russian Convoy Club continued to keep going. We are the London and Home Counties branch, with most of our members coming from the London area, and we meet once a month at the Royal British Legion at Kennington, which lets us have a room for free, although we try to make up for that by having a good drink.

In 2011, Gordon Long decided that he wanted to get up a private trip to return to Russia. A few of the chaps said that they would like to go with him, but I had to say that I couldn't manage it. The cost was one thousand two hundred pounds each – two thousand four hundred pounds for me and Di – and, even if you can obtain travel insurance, it is extremely expensive for somebody of my age. I told Gordon that, much as we'd like to, unfortunately, we wouldn't be able to join the trip.

With a few members of the club, I was invited to a reception at the Russian Embassy in London. I had been to a few of these functions over the previous few years, although I had never got used to being greeted by a line of people and having to walk along it to shake hands with everybody.

We were standing around chatting, and I was introduced to a Scottish chap, Andy MacGill, who was married to a Belarusian girl and who had some business interests in Russia. Somebody had told him about the club's proposed trip, and he asked me whether I would be going. I told that I couldn't afford it, but, not to worry, I had been there in 2005 and thoroughly enjoyed it.

He asked me how much the trip cost and, when I told him, he said, 'Don't worry, I'll pay it for you'. I'd only spoken to him for five minutes, and here he was offering to pay for both me and Di to go, which would set him back over two thousand pounds!

It was a terrific offer, but I left the reception without seeing him again and I thought that would probably be the last I heard from him. A couple of days later, he contacted me to find out who he should send the money to. It was absolutely smashing of him to do it – how many people would do that for somebody they had met only the once, and then just for a few minutes?

Andy said that he was keen to meet up with our group in Arkhangelsk. Unfortunately, he had a very bad car crash in Belarus and nearly died. He spent several months in hospital.

JAMES PITTS

CHAPTER TWENTY-FIVE

My second trip to Russia in six years was for eleven days, and it was quite a lot more relaxed and informal than the previous one, although the Russians were just as warm and friendly towards us.

Gordon had plenty of contacts and he laid on a great itinerary in co-operation with some different groups in Russia. They provided us with a couple of translators who were students, very pretty girls with great senses of humour. We were driven around in a couple of vehicles, a coach on which the majority travelled and an old blue mini-bus, in which Di and I sat with Ernie Kennedy, Gerry (from Wales) and his partner Maureen, a retired Mayoress from Pembroke Dock, and a couple of the young Russian girls.

We had so much fun on our bus, joking around and singing so many songs, that it was quickly nicknamed the 'naughty bus'. We became quite friendly with the Russian girls and one of them, Alexandra, subsequently twice came to England to stay with Di and I.

We were again treated terrifically in Murmansk and Arkhangelsk, where they laid on another lot of functions for us. Everywhere we went, we were given books, most of which were hardbacks. At one memorial, a lady came up to me and held out a book for me to take. Through an interpreter, she said that she had been a little girl during the war but that her parents and grandparents had told her the history of the convoys and how they helped to prevent their family from starving to death. She said that she had never forgotten the stories and that she had passed them onto her own children and grandchildren. As she gave me the book, she wept, and I embraced her.

A retired Russian Army captain and his wife visited us at our hotel several times. We nicknamed the man 'Mr Watch' because he carried around with him a number of wrist watches that he gifted to any veteran to whom he took a liking. One evening, he took off a watch from his wrist, and handed it to me. I had nothing of worth to give him in return, so Di took off a Swordfish brooch from her jacket and gave it to his wife, who seemed thrilled with the gift. We met this couple at many of the functions that we attended, and we became quite friendly with them.

For most of the time, we ate at official functions. But when we were around the hotel at lunchtime, Alexandra took us to one of the local snack bars, where she explained exactly what food was available, ordered it for us (she said in case they tried to overcharge us) and collected the money from each of us to pay for it. That was a nice experience because we were able to try out different Russian foods, some of it quite similar to the food we had enjoyed on our visits to Leona's family in the Czech Republic. Alexandra also took us to the shopping malls so that we could buy gifts and mementoes to take home with us.

We visited a school where the children were either orphaned or unable to live at home for a variety of reasons. The school was in an old house that had been converted, and they had done a nice job of it. All the children wore a junior naval uniform, and it was touching to watch them perform a few songs and a play for us. At its conclusion, as we were leaving the hall, a young girl, aged about thirteen, ran across to Di and threw her arms around her, saying in broken English, ' I like you the best'. I asked her what her name was and she said Lisa, but we didn't have time to speak to her for any length of time because we were escorted off in different directions.

A couple of days later, we visited a memorial to lay some flowers in memory of those killed in the war, which was something we were frequently asked to do. A large gathering of students were in a group watching us from behind a barrier when we saw Lisa duck under it and run towards us. She threw her arms around both Di and I. A teacher summoned her away, and, after the ceremony we tried to locate her, but the children must have been taken away quite quickly.

Di was very moved by the girl and asked Alexandra to help her track her down so that, perhaps, we could write to her. Unfortunately, Alexandra was unable to discover her whereabouts.

One of the functions was attended by Valya Golysheva, a university lecturer who had written a number of books in her native Russian about the war. I had got to know her a little because she had been to London previously to interview members of our club for an educational book that she had been writing for students about the convoys. I had stood back, so I didn't appear in this book, but when I met her this time she asked me to tell her about my experiences, and she said that I would be in her next book.

We stayed a few days in St Petersburg, a wonderful city, and went to the British consulate and the American consulate, where we were treated to a wonderful meal and, as always seemed to be the way, unlimited alcohol.

We were invited to a reception hosted by Valentina Matviyenko, the Governor of St Petersburg, at Mariinsky Palace,[70] a building which had once belonged to the Tsar. It was the most incredible palace, full of gold and jewels, and it had a solid gold horse-drawn coach and huge ornate gardens that led down to a lake.

I said to Di, it was no wonder that the people had risen up against the Tsar when they had been so hungry and he'd had all this luxury.

CHAPTER TWENTY-SIX

Our campaign for the Arctic Star received a boost when the Daily Mail newspaper took up our cause and argued for the Government to change its stance.

During their campaigning ahead of the 2010 general election, a number of Conservative candidates had promised us that, should they be elected, they would see to it that we were given the medal. However, once they were in power, some of them seemed to find reasons to not keep to that promise.

It seemed that our campaign had run out of steam, but it received a most unlikely shot in the arm when Andrew Robathan, the minister responsible for veterans, stood up in the House of Commons and compared our request for a medal to that of the large number of honours that had been 'thrown around' by dictators such as Colonel Gaddafi (Libya) and Saddam Hussein (Iraq).[71]

I was at the Commons to hear him make this unnecessary comparison, and, on reflection, I felt that this was the moment when the Daily Mail went into battle on our behalf. Caroline

Dinenage,[72] a Conservative MP for Portsmouth, had organised a Parliamentary debate in which she urged the Government to keep its promise to us. Along with Cdr Grenfell and myself, six other members of our club had been invited to attend the debate.

When she spoke, she was very complimentary about us and she said that it was only just and right that we be awarded a campaign medal.

But when Robathan stood up to speak in reply, he pooh-poohed our claim, saying that Britain wasn't like Libya, Iraq and North Korea in dishing out medals all over the place. Some of our chaps became quite irate over that, but it got even worse when he said the words, 'We have taken the view in this country, traditionally, that medals will only be awarded for campaigns that show risk and rigour.'

Cdr Grenfell was livid, and the consensus among us was that this Robathan chap obviously had no idea of the sacrifices that had been made by those serving on the Arctic Convoys. As he continued to speak, there was a bit more of a hoo-ha among our chaps, and I had to help quieten down one or two of them because they had become so loud in their protests that they had attracted the attention of the Commons ushers, who thereafter kept a watchful eye on our gang of feisty octogenarians.

The irony was that his uncomplimentary words probably did more to get us the medal than anything else that had happened previously. The Daily Mail had a reporter at the debate, and his story the next day was full of criticism of what was said – Miss Dinenage said that Robathan's words were 'extremely ill-judged', the Labour party called them 'a slap in the face', Cdr Grenfell was interviewed and said that Robathan should be sacked and Simon Weston, the Falklands war veteran, accused him of making a 'terrible insult' and taking 'a cheap shot'. I almost felt sorry for Robathan.

I had liked the way in which Miss Dinenage had spoken during the debate. Without being dramatic, she had reminded the Prime Minister, David Cameron, of the promises made before the election and explained that these needed to be honoured as quickly as possible because our numbers were dwindling by the month.

Afterwards, she told us that her local newspaper in Portsmouth, The News, had organised a petition in our support. Apparently, forty-six thousand people had signed it, which was humbling to hear.

Robathan did issue an apology of sorts, saying that he was 'making the point that we honour people for their service in a very different way to that of authoritarian regimes', although it seemed to me that he was more interested in trying to justify his words than actually saying sorry.

I didn't get too upset about it because I know that there will always be people who are happy to speak without thinking too deeply about what comes out of their mouth. But some of the other chaps were very angry, and I think it fired Cdr Grenfell up to be even more determined (if that was possible) to get us the medal.

The Russian media also picked up on our campaign, and they often had articles on their English language TV and radio stations, as well as various websites, about the Government's reluctance to give us the medal. Even the president, Vladimir Putin, spoke out on the matter and said that he wanted us to be given the very notable Russian honour, the Medal of Ushakov, but that he was being opposed by the Foreign Office. Apparently, the argument was that acceptance of the medal would break the rules governing awards for British servicemen.

It was all a bit Catch-22, with the Foreign Office saying that we could not have the Medal of Ushakov because we had already been recognised with the award of the Atlantic Star, but we felt that the Atlantic Star was not truly representative of our role in the war, and the Government did not seem to have the desire to give us the requested Arctic Star. Some of the chaps became quite upset when they learned that veterans from countries including Canada, Australia and America had been given permission by their respective governments to accept the Medal of Ushakov.

As I had expected, Cdr Grenfell fumed at the injustice of it. He wrote to the Government to point out that the Medal of Ushakov was a medal for valour, not a campaign medal, and, when he got nowhere with that, he asked the Russians to unilaterally award it to us, although that was something they were not, at that stage, willing to do, even though the Russian Embassy in London issued a statement saying that the Foreign Office's decision was a matter of 'deep regret' and urging a change of position.

A few of the British newspapers, in particular the Mail, continued to speak out about our campaign, and I think, in the end, the Government probably got a bit fed up with it all. Although nothing moves quickly in such circles, we were told by various people that it was increasingly likely that we would, eventually, be awarded the Arctic Star.

I seemed to be becoming something of a regular at Buckingham Palace garden parties, and on 24th May, 2012, I was presented to the Duchess of Gloucester.

Di and I, along with the others to meet her, were sat apart from the rest of the people attending the function. It was an extremely hot day, the sun was blazing, and we had to sit in a row of chairs in the open for an hour and quarter to wait for her to work her way along the line of people. She finally got to us, she was pleasant enough, and, as soon as we'd had our little chat, we were free to go and look for something to eat and drink. However, all the refreshment marquees seemed to have closed.

We finally spotted one that was still open, but the chap on the door was, I felt, unnecessarily offhand towards us and wouldn't let us enter the marquee. He told us that we needed a voucher to enter, so we went off and found the Lft-Colonel who had organised our line-up for the Duchess. He gave us a voucher, but this time the jobsworth said that only one of us could go in because we had only the one voucher.

We were both hot and thirsty, so I went back to the Lft-Colonel and explained what was happening. He said that he didn't have any more vouchers, so he marched over to address the doorman and told him in a very authoritative tone, 'I don't care how many vouchers you say they've got to have – you let them in to get a drink.' The doorman stood aside without argument.

In the autumn, I went to a reception at the Russian Embassy in London, where a fair amount of the conversation was about whether we would be given the Arctic Star. I was introduced to a chap who seemed very interested in my wartime experiences, and he spoke to me for about twenty minutes about the convoys. He said that he felt that we should be given the medal, and he said to me, 'If you don't hear anything about it, let me know and I'll do what I can.'

He gave me his card, and I saw that his name was Baron Soley of Hammersmith. However, I didn't have any need to make contact with him because only a few weeks after this reception it was announced that we were to be given the Arctic Star.

Fittingly, Cdr Grenfell was among the first veterans to receive his.

Unfortunately, he'd had a heart attack and was too ill to attend a ceremony on HMS Belfast at which David Cameron gave some medals to a few veterans, but a special function was staged in Portsmouth, where the Chief of Defence Staff, General Sir David Richards, presented Cdr Grenfell with his medal. He died only three months after receiving it.

Without his efforts, I don't know whether the Government would ever have agreed to the Arctic Star. As he had pointed out when the Government's change of heart was first announced, many men who should have received the medal had died in the time it had taken for our request to be answered.

For many years I had marched at the Cenotaph on Remembrance Sunday, initially with the air-gunners association and then with the Russian Convoy Club after the air-gunners had got too old to carry on. People who watch the commemorations on television don't get to see what a tiring and demanding day it can be, especially if the weather is not kind, and we had decided previously to make the march on 11th November, 2012, our final one.

However, in 2013 we were asked to march for one more time in memory of Cdr Grenfell, and we were honoured to do that. Cdr Grenfell's daughter, Trudie, joined us, and I think that meant something to his family.

But that had to be the last time because we're all too old – even on that march, four out of the twelve were in wheelchairs.

All things must come to an end, and we kept it going for as long as we possibly could. In the final few years of the air-gunners, our numbers fell away so much that some of the veterans' relatives joined with us to give us a presence. On one occasion, when there was only five of us air-gunners, we were picked out on BBC television. David Dimbleby commented, 'If you look up in the sky and imagine a small aircraft flying along with an open place behind the pilot, that is where the air-gunners used to sit – it certainly was the loneliest position in the world'.

For my final march with the air-gunners, I was asked whether

I could obtain a wreath to lay at the Cenotaph. I contacted Gordon Long at the Russian Convoy Club, who purchased one on our behalf. I designed and made a badge to fit into the centre of the wreath, and I laid this at the memorial.

When I say that the day is tiring and demanding, I don't want to be seen as complaining, just that, when you get to nearly ninety years of age, your body finds it more difficult to do what it once did so easily. There was a lot of standing around, and I was on my feet from early in the morning until well into the afternoon.

A typical day started with me leaving home in time to arrive at Horse Guard's Parade by 9.30am. We were given passes to show our column number and, over the years, friendships were formed between the various columns – you might line up next to the Gurkhas or an airforce regiment or the Home Guard. Many veterans took hip flasks of whisky or rum and shared these around while we stood waiting to set off.

Before marching, we would be taken into Whitehall to watch on giant TV screens the Queen and other dignitaries pay their respects.

We wouldn't start to march until well after most of the dignitaries had departed, and the waiting around could be quite hard, especially when it was cold and my legs seemed to lock up. But I always appreciated the incredible atmosphere, with huge crowds there to cheer and clap us, and I was proud to march in memory of those we had lost. I would think of Henry, my friend and fellow air-gunner, and wonder about the man he would have become had he not been lost in the waters of Boston harbour.

Over the years, various members of my family came to watch me march and, for the last one, Chris insisted on accompanying me in case I needed support. He saw that I was coping okay, so he assisted a good mate of mine, Jimmy Wells, another Russian Convoy Club member, whose grandson Neil was there to help him as well. As I said, several of our members were being pushed in wheelchairs, and the few of us marching behind them could barely keep up – gaps kept occurring between the lines!

I was interviewed by The Times and a picture of me marching with Chris alongside me was used in the newspaper – people kept asking me who the old guy was standing beside me!

Over the years, I marched in rain, fog, sleet and glorious sunshine. The march itself only took around thirty minutes, but it was something of a challenge after all the standing around.

I still wanted to commemorate the day, and, on 9th November, 2014, I attended a ceremony at the Imperial War Museum with a few other veterans. It was quite a moving experience, as we were taken to the front of a crowd of people at the museum for a two minute silence before walking to the Russian memorial in Geraldine Park, where the Russian Convoy Club chairman, Ernie Davies, and I laid a wreath, and Stan Ballard, the deputy chairman, read the Epitaph. I hope that we'll be able to continue doing this for at least a few more years.

CHAPTER TWENTY-SEVEN

I received my Arctic Star with the minimum of fuss. It arrived through the post with only a brief letter to inform me that I had qualified for the award. A few of the chaps from my branch of the Russian Convoy Club also received their medals in this manner, and some of them were a little miffed about that, although there was nothing we could do about it and I felt that we shouldn't be seen to be ungrateful.

Anyway, I only had my medal for three months before I agreed to give it away.

A few years previously, at a function aboard HMS Belfast, I had met a chap, Eugene Kasevin, a Russian, who described himself as an 'entrepreneur' and who worked out of The Russia House in London. He had organised the function as part of the Victory Day[73] celebrations in London.

Like a lot of Russian people, he seemed genuinely interested in the convoy veterans and he organised a few social functions and trips for us, obtaining money from different organisations in this country and Russia to finance the events.

He is very keen on promoting good relations between

177

Britain and Russia, and I became quite friendly with him – he was happy to help us out whenever he could. He had become involved with the campaign to get us the Medal of Ushakov, and, through his connections in Moscow, set about organising a trip for veterans from our club to visit the Russian capital to present one of our Arctic Star medals to the Central Museum of the Great Patriotic War.[74]

He somehow got the finances together to pay for our flights and accommodation, and arranged for us to travel over in late autumn. Somebody from the club said that they would get a duplicate of the medal made to take to Russia, but Eugene got in touch with me through Di to explain that the museum would not accept a replica – it had to be a veteran's medal or nothing. Eugene said that he wondered whether anybody would give up their medal after the prolonged fight we'd had to secure it, and, therefore, the trip might be cancelled.

Di asked me whether I would be prepared to donate my medal to the museum. I didn't really want to give it up, but for the sake of everybody involved I said that I would do that. Eugene made plans for my medal to be shipped to Russia ahead of our visit, his idea being that it should follow the same sea route from Britain to Russia as we had taken during the war.

While these plans were being made, our club was contacted by somebody from Russia who asked whether any of us veterans would be prepared to fly to Arkhangelsk to carry the Olympic torch as part of its relay ahead of the 2014 Winter Olympics in Sochi.[75] We were told that the organisers felt that it would be nice if one of us could represent Great Britain, and that it would give the people of Arkhangelsk another opportunity to acknowledge the role of the convoys.

A couple of the chaps in our club were asked, but they turned it down because they felt that they were too old for such an endeavour. I'm not sure how my name got thrown into the ring, but I was asked whether I would be willing to do it, and I thought that it sounded quite an interesting adventure and that it could be something that my grandchildren would enjoy me doing.

I was told that I could take somebody with me as a carer, but Di said that she didn't want to go because we had builders working at our house. They were putting up a two-storey extension to the side of our house, something that Chris had proposed and financed because he was concerned that, as Di and I got older, we would have difficulty in getting up and down the stairs.

The plan was for an additional room downstairs that we could make into a bedroom when necessary, plus a shower room and toilet, while upstairs we would have another bedroom. It was a big job and the builders were making quite a mess, so Di decided that she didn't want to leave the house with all this going on.

After thirty years of working, Chris had started full-time university that September, but he said that he would come with me on the trip, which, with the travelling, would be for five days. The British Embassy in Moscow helped sort out all the formalities.

I went to represent the Royal Navy while another chap, Charles Downs, represented the Merchant Navy. I had recently marked my eighty-ninth birthday, and Charles was of a similar age.

We flew out from Heathrow to St Petersburg, where we were met at the airport by a man who had once been the commander of a Russian nuclear submarine and who worked for the Russian government as a liaison between them and us.

The flight to Arkhangelsk departed from a separate airport, so he drove us across the city and helped us check-in for the internal flight. He was good to have around because he had a lot of clout and got me through security even though I was wearing my blazer with my medals. That was something I was grateful for because in recent years I have found airports quite problematic. I understand why they need to be strict, but, at my age, taking off my jacket, belt and shoes is not as easy as it once was – and getting them back on can be even more of a problem!

We were met in Arkhangelsk by Acting Lft-Commander Adrian Coghill, a naval attaché at the British Embassy in Moscow. I had met him on our first visit to Russia in 2005 when he was a Chief Petty Officer on the Sutherland. He could speak Russian and had been promoted to naval attaché at the embassy, although he has since returned to England to run one of the naval bases at Portsmouth.

Adrian is a smashing chap and he got on really well with the Russians. On my trips, I had witnessed a lot of respect between the naval personnel of both countries. There seemed to be a lot of comradeship and understanding, with little or no animosity. Indeed, the former commander of the nuclear submarine told us that people would probably be surprised at how closely our respective navies liaised at times.

Charles travelled to Arkhangelsk with a friend, John, and they joined Chris, Adrian and I for dinner and a few drinks on our first evening. Actually, it was more than a few drinks and I was glad to have Chris there to help me back to our room!

We were up early the next morning, the day of carrying the torch, and were taken to a reception in the city centre where we met everybody else who was to take part in the procession.[75] We were briefed about what we should and should not do, basic information such as when our individual flame would be lit and by whom, and who to hand your torch over to at the end of your stint – and who to definitely not hand your torch over to!

We were told that each of us would carry the flame for a

distance of approximately three hundred metres. They presented us with our uniforms – jacket, trousers, hat and gloves – and gave us each a number. I had the number fifty-six.

There was a big celebration in the city centre, with lots of singing and dancing. The people seemed very happy to have the Olympic torch in their city, and a big crowd turned out to watch. It was a cold morning, but were lucky in that it wasn't snowing.

We boarded a coach to be taken along the route of the torch, with each of us to be dropped off at our designated points. The torch bearers were sat at the front of the coach, while our carers/relatives/friends took their seats towards the back.

I was the first in my group to be dropped off in a street a short distance from the city centre. Chris was chatting to somebody at the back of the coach and didn't see me get off, and it was only after a few more people had been offloaded that he realised that I was no longer on the vehicle. He had to stop the coach and run back to where I was doing my bit, all the time worried that he would miss it – the security people kept stopping him to ask him why he was running!

Other than that, the whole thing was very well organised. I got off the coach to be met by a couple of volunteers. As I stood waiting for my turn, the weather seemed to turn a little colder and it started to snow. Fortunately, the suit they had given me to wear was very warm.

I was handed my torch by one of the organisers, who lit it for me and told me that he would tell me when I should set off. I was surprised at the heavy weight of it and I needed two hands to hold it. Adrian asked me to carry a small union flag, so I asked him to stick that in my clenched hands. He put it in just the right place so that people could see both it and the torch.

Many of those scheduled to carry the torch after me were clearly younger and fitter than I was. We were told that we could hold it in one hand above our head and that we could jog, although I'm afraid both of those were beyond me. As I set off at a pace a little faster than my typical walking pace (lots of adrenalin!), it began to snow a little more and the wind picked up, blowing my flame around. I prayed that it wouldn't go out.

There was a big crowd of people lining the streets, and they were tremendous to me. Everybody was clapping, and once my union flag was spotted they seemed to chant in unison, saying over and over, 'Great Britain, Great Britain'. I could see Adrian was happy with that.

Three hundred metres was plenty far enough for me, and I was puffing a bit by the time I got to the next bearer, an attractive young woman. I had to use my torch to light hers, and, with a bit of help, I managed that.

Each bearer was given the opportunity to buy the torch that they had carried. They cost the equivalent of around two hundred and sixty pounds, and the Russians must have thought them a decent investment because they jumped at the chance. My torch was purchased by Adrian for the British Embassy in Moscow, where I was told that it would be put on display.

Charles was around six places further down the line. After our group of carriers had each had their turned, the coach returned to collect us and take us to a concert in a hall. It was packed solid, but I still had my suit on and they made room for me, although Chris had a bit of a job to get close to me. When we were getting ready for dinner that evening, Chris surprised me by asking whether he could wear my medals – apparently he was quite jealous of the attention that I had received from a number of pretty young girls and decided he wanted a bit of that!

The following day was a bit more relaxed. We were taken to

a couple of schools to talk to the children about the convoys, and Charles, being a retired headmaster, seemed to greatly enjoy that.

I had done this a few times on previous visits, and each time I visited a school I was touched by the respect shown to us by the children. In Britain, the convoys are not such a big part of our history, but for the Russian people, and especially for those in places close to the sea like Arkhangelsk, anything and everything about the convoys is of great importance and interest. It's hard to draw comparisons, but they look on the convoys in perhaps a similar way to how we in Britain think of the Battle of Britain and those airmen who defied the odds.

We spent quite some time talking to the children, and returned to our hotel for an evening meal with Adrian, who seemed very happy with how our trip had gone. We had each been interviewed by Russian television, and we were happy to put over the message that we had been delighted to represent Great Britain on such a memorable occasion.

On our return, we were again met at St Petersburg by the former nuclear submarine commander, who oversaw our airport transfers and made sure that we got on the flight back to London without hassle.

My family back home had followed the event as much as they could on television, in the newspapers and on the internet. They were bemused to see the Winter Olympics official website report that torch-bearers had included a 'British explorer Jamie Pitts – a veteran of several Arctic expeditions – who was invited to carry the Olympic flame due to his affinity with the region'.

When I returned home, they questioned me about whether I had met this man (who, incidentally, had the same name as my third grandchild, Steve's eldest boy), but, of course, I had no idea who he was.

Steve did his best to try to track him down but without success, so we still don't know whether there was a third British torch-bearer in Arkhangelsk on that day or whether somebody in the Olympic movement had got themselves in a bit of a muddle and mistook an eighty-nine-year-old former air-gunner for a renown British explorer! (although I did get to see a fair bit of the world while serving in the Fleet Air Arm.)

The British Embassy in Moscow sent out a press release saying that 'the participation of British veterans...in Arkhangelsk's celebrations reminds us of the historic partnership between the UK and Russia. It also demonstrates that our two countries have much in common in the modern era.'

I was happy to be part of anything that might make people think a little more of what we have in common rather than try to make mischief from our differences.

CHAPTER TWENTY-EIGHT

I had only been back in the UK for a couple of days when I went to HMS Belfast[76] to hand over my Arctic Star medal for the start of its journey to Moscow.

I'd had some second thoughts about giving up the medal, primarily because it meant that I could not wear it with my other medals, but, having made a promise, I could not back down.

On the Belfast, we had a nice ceremony at which several of the chaps from our club were joined by the First Sea Lord, Sir Alan West, Simon Hughes, the MP, and some officials from the Belfast and the Russian Embassy.

One of my fellow club members, Stan Ballard, had made a casing for the medal, and I put my Arctic Star in that and handed it to Eugene. We had a good drink-up.

The following day, the medal was taken to Sheerness, where Eugene presented it to Hannu Soinila, captain of the ship M/S Linda, to be taken by sea to St Petersburg. Although the plan had been to send the medal on the same route as that of the convoys, it actually went through the North Sea, Baltic

Sea and the Gulf of Finland. The journey was given the codename 'CG' in memory of Cdr Grenfell.

It arrived a week later and was officially accepted at the British Consulate in St Petersburg by British naval attaché Captain David Fields. He took it to the British Embassy in Moscow, where it was held until the official presentation ceremony at the museum on 29th November.

Di had missed my trip to carry the Olympic flame a month previously, but I was keen for her to join me in Moscow, so we sorted things out at home so that she could also travel.

Apart from me, there were seven other veterans flying out – Stan Ballard, Tony Snelling, Ernie Davies, Jimmy Wells, Frank Bond, David Kennedy and Fred Udell. Ernie Kennedy had also been due to join us, but he had a problem with his back shortly before we departed and he had to stay at home.

The trip was quite a big thing, and ITN sent a news reporter, Luke Hanrahan, and a camerawoman, Gemma Creely, to film the trip, while the violinist Litsa Tunnah also joined us.

Unfortunately, the weather in Moscow was much harsher than it had been only a few weeks previously in Arkhangelsk. We arrived in temperatures of minus five or six degrees centigrade, and there was also a strong wind chill. It was a cold that seemed more severe than anything we ever had back home, and whenever we ventured out of the hotel you felt the chill very quickly.

On the morning of the ceremony, we were invited to visit Tim Barrow, the British Ambassador, at his residence. This was situated on the embankment opposite the Kremlin and had some spectacular views. From there, we were taken by minibus to the Central Museum of the Great Patriotic War, which really is something else. It's so big that I couldn't begin to guess at its size, but we were told that around one million people visit it each year. Apparently, construction on it started in the days of communism, but it was only completed during the presidency of Boris Yeltsin in 1995.

The organisers pushed out the red carpet for us. We were introduced to some Russian veterans, and we were asked to lay flowers at the Monument of Sorrow, which was a sculpture of a mother crying over the body of her dead son. We had a minute's silence to remember all those who had died during the war. It's almost beyond comprehension, but nobody should ever forget that around twenty-four million Russians were killed during the war, which was around one in six of their entire population.

While we were waiting for the official ceremony to begin, I kept being asked to do interviews for the numerous Russian television and radio stations that were covering the event. I was taken away several times by different people to talk to TV presenters in their studios. They all asked pretty much the same questions about the convoys and why I was in Moscow to donate my Arctic Star medal, but then one of them asked who had accompanied me on my journey to Moscow. I pointed out Di, so somebody went over to get her and she had to talk live on Russian television. I thought she did very well, although she didn't go much on it and told me not to point her out again!

The ceremony itself started with a speech from the deputy director of the museum, Mikhail Mikhalchev, who read out a letter from the Queen in which she said that she recognised the historic importance to Russia of the medal and sent her best wishes to all us veterans.

The museum's director, Vladimir Zaborovskiy, gave quite a long speech praising us veterans and the convoys, and David Fields gave his thanks to us and spoke about the close friendship that historically had existed between the Royal Navy and the Russian Navy. This was something that I had previously been told about, and I have no problem with it because I think us and the Russian people have more in common than is sometimes portrayed by politicians and the media. Surely, it's better to talk and co-operate than it is to be at each other's throats.

Having lived through the war and the Cold War, I feel we must do everything we possibly can to make sure that future generations do not have to endure conflict in any shape or form.

Because it was my medal that was being handed over, I had anticipated that I might be asked to say a few words. Before we had left home, Di had told me to make some notes of what I might say in the event of me being called upon to speak, but I told her that I wasn't going to do that. I explained that, should I try to read from notes, I'd get myself in such a muddle that it would be embarrassing for everybody. I decided that, should a speech be required, I'd just ad-lib a few words.

There was a few hundred people in the Hall of Glory, virtually all of them in rows of chairs looking directly at me, which was a bit shaky. I hadn't done anything before even remotely close to addressing such a large and distinguished gathering, but, as I feared, I was asked to speak.

I'm not a man of words and I was nervous, but I thought I did quite well. I spoke about the huge cost of the war, the immense suffering and grief that it had caused, the sacrifices that had been made and why the convoys had been needed. It had been a tough decision for me to give up my medal, but I told the audience that it was an honour for me to present it to the museum and the Russian people because of all the hardships that they had endured. I finished by saying that I hoped that, one day, my grandchildren would be able to travel to Moscow to see my Arctic Star on display. As I spoke, a translator stood alongside me to relay my words in Russian.

There wasn't really anything else for me to say, and I was relieved to get away from the podium.

Eugene gave a brief description of the medal's journey from London to Moscow, and then us veterans stood in a line and passed the medal along it until I got to hand it over to Mr Zaborovskiy. We had a bit of a manly hug and he said that it had been accepted as one of the museum's most precious and historic displays. He said that the medal would be on permanent show in the main section of the museum.

There was some music and songs, with Stan taking the microphone to sing his own version of a song called The Way We Were. The Russians seemed to enjoy it.

To round off the ceremony, we were each presented with a medal by the Russian Orthodox Church. We were given the Order of Saint Righteous Grand Duke Dmitry Donskoy, a high honour that they give only to people who they feel have shown exceptional bravery. Only around one thousand have ever been issued, and my number is nine hundred and fifty-six.

It was a nice day, but we were on our feet for a long time and we all found it quite tiring.

The following morning, a Saturday, the last day of November, we were taken by minibus to the Eternal Flame at the Tomb of the Unknown Soldier, which is alongside the Kremlin Wall. The plan was for us to lay red carnations in memory of all those who had been lost in the war, but when we approached the memorial we were told that we didn't have permission to lay the flowers.

The weather was bitterly cold, and, while Eugene went off with a couple of Russian officials to try to get it sorted out for us to lay the flowers, we had to stand around for nearly an hour. It was too cold for people of our age to be outdoors in those temperatures for such a long time, and Tony Snelling, a year older than me, became so unwell that he had to be held up to stop him from collapsing to the pavement. He was clearly not in a very good way, shivering and pale. Somebody got on their phone to call for an ambulance and, while we waited for it to arrive, Luke Hanrahan took off his coat and lay that on Tony, while Di took off the Russian-styled hat she had been wearing and put that on his head.

Before being taken off to hospital, Tony still summoned the determination to stand up and lay his flowers at the memorial.

We were due to fly home the next day, but Tony was diagnosed with pneumonia and kept in a hospital for a week. We flew home without him, with Eugene staying behind in Moscow to help care for him.

When Tony was discharged, the hospital handed Eugene a bill for his treatment, which ran to quite a few thousand pounds. Eugene said that he didn't know how he was going to pay for it, so he asked his friend Peter Hambro, a British businessman, who apparently said no more than, 'How do I pay it?' We had met Peter on several occasions aboard HMS Belfast and elsewhere, as his company is one of the principal sponsors of the Victory Day celebrations in London each May.

Tony flew home seven days after us. Eugene accompanied him on the flight to continue his care of him and, thankfully, Tony made a decent recovery.

That trip was a privilege to have been on, but it took a lot out of us all. After I returned home, I was very poorly until well into the following year, having also been diagnosed with pneumonia, while Stan also felt terrible. Stan can be quite a character, and, when I met up with him again after we were both feeling a little better, he joked that Eugene had gone close to killing off three of the eight veterans who had travelled to Russia – a ratio that the Germans had failed to achieve during the war!

Membership of our branch of the Russian Convoy Club had continued to fall away. Gordon Long, our secretary for twenty-odd years, decided that it was time that he stood down from the post, and I thought that might be the end of the club – we had occasionally spoken about how the club could possibly fold when his time was up.

All of us wanted to keep it going, but being secretary is a time-consuming and demanding role, and there always seems to be something to organise, correspondence to answer, newsletters, minutes, meetings. Nobody was forthcoming, so I asked Di whether she would consider taking on the job. She agreed, although I think she has had cause to regret it a few times since!

Having consented to us being awarded the Arctic Star, the Government also agreed that we could be presented with the Medal of Ushakov. Putin, who I understood had continued to push for the Russians to be given permission to make the award, flew to London to present a handful of veterans with their medals at a ceremony with Cameron.

It was decided that no medals would be awarded posthumously.

I was interviewed by the television station Russia Today about how I felt about being nominated to receive the medal, which really is quite something because it is Russia's highest naval award and is named after an admiral who apparently never lost a single ship, let alone a battle, in forty-three engagements in the eighteenth century!

I had been on television and radio quite a lot over the previous couple of years and I was a bit more comfortable in talking to a camera or microphone.

I said: 'Unfortunately, we can't all go on forever, but I'm so happy that I have lived long enough to have this honour. It is important that recognition goes to the people. It will give me great pride to wear it.'

Okay, that was hardly Churchillian, but for me, where I had come from, I thought I spoke okay.

In a nice touch, Eugene organised for twenty veterans to receive their medals in a ceremony on HMS Belfast. This took place on 9th May, 2014, and there were nineteen of us present. I can give you their names (in alphabetical order) – Stan Ballard, Cyril Banks, Frank Bond, Austin Byrne, Harry Card, Ernest Davies, Charles Erswell, Alan Florence, Albert Foulser, John Hirst, Arthur Hutton, David Kennedy, Ernest Kennedy, Arthur Lauricks, Leslie Perks, Anthony Snelling, Fred Udell and Arthur Waddington. Unfortunately, Gordon Long was unwell and unable to attend.

Eugene read out a message from the Queen wishing us a 'successful and memorable occasion', and Lord David Richards, a former head of the British Armed Forces, gave a speech in which he was complimentary about us.

We were presented with the medal by the Russian chargé d'affaires, Alexander Kramarenko, in the presence of some dignitaries from Britain and Russia. When it was my turn to receive my medal, I told Mr Kramarenko that I had presented my Arctic Star to the museum in Moscow, and he said that he knew all about that.

After a minute's silence to remember the lost, followed by eleven salutes from the Belfast's four-inch guns, we got stuck into the alcohol with rum and vodka toasts, then Di and I were given something else to celebrate.

Our granddaughter Amy, who is Steve's second daughter, was due to give birth to her second child and had been taken into hospital in Northampton that morning. Di was a bit on edge waiting for news, and when she got the message that Amy had given birth to a healthy baby boy she was very happy. She mentioned it to Eugene, who silenced the room by tapping a glass and announced the news of the new arrival – everybody cheered (even Mr Kramarenko!), and that was quite something for us. We were having a good drink anyway, but that was another reason to raise a glass!

I was happy for Di because she had been given quite a lot of grief over this event. Being our secretary, a lot of the arrangements for the day had been made through her, and she had worked hard to get the veterans organised and ready. But because of the size of the rooms on the Belfast, numbers were limited and some people simply weren't willing to accept that. Di did her best to accommodate them all, but it was impossible to keep everybody happy and there was a bit of gatecrashing, which Eugene got some stick about from the people who run the Belfast.

Eugene had some sort of public relations role with a group called the Friends of North Caucasus[77] and, on 16th June, 2014, they organised a reception at the House of Lords in London, hosted by Lord Ahmed.

Di and I were invited as 'guests of honour' and we arrived to find around one hundred VIPs from British, Russian and international businesses, diplomats and representatives of the media, culture and education. It was quite some gathering.

I had been told to turn up wearing my medals, although I had to leave a space for where the Arctic Star should have been. I had been given a replica, but obviously I could not pin this to my blazer.

Di and I sat at the top table. When we were introduced to the other guests, everybody in the room stood up and applauded, and I wasn't quite sure how to react. I was only glad that I wasn't called upon to give a speech.

The North Caucasus is a long way from Murmansk, being

closer to the Middle East than it is to the north Russian coast, but it seemed even these people were knowledgeable about the convoys and wanted to show their appreciation of them.

CHAPTER TWENTY-NINE

After our difficulty with getting a drink at our previous garden party at Buckingham Palace, Di and I had agreed that we probably shouldn't attend any more. However, we received an invitation to attend a garden party on 26th June, 2014, at which I would be presented to either the Queen or the Duke of York, and we agreed that we would like to go.

This was another event organised by The Not Forgotten Association, and the idea was that some of us would be presented to the Queen and the rest to the Duke of York.

I was put in the group to meet the Duke of York. We were organised into smaller groups of four or five, and an official asked each of us for a few details about ourselves so that he could inform the Duke who we were and what we had done.

Chairs had been laid out, so we sat down and waited for the Duke to work his way down the line, accompanied by David Cowley, the vice-chairman of the Not Forgotten Association, and Rosie Thompson, its head of events. Di and the other partners/carers were sat in chairs behind us.

When the Duke got to us, those of us who were capable of getting up out of chairs stood up. The chap who had asked for some information to feed to the prince didn't have his paperwork to hand, so I told Prince Andrew that I had been on the Arctic Convoys as an air-gunner and that I had met him in Russia in 2005 for the commemorations to mark the sixtieth anniversary of the end of the war.

I doubted that he could remember me, and he meets so many people in the course of his duties that this was hardly a surprise. I spoke to him for four or five minutes, telling him about how I had survived three plane crashes, and he seemed interested in those experiences, although, to be fair, listening to such stories is just a day's work for him.

The chap sitting next to me was unable to get up, so he didn't get much conversation with the Duke. I felt a bit sorry for him, but that's how it goes.

This was another event at which Di had some problems with the family of one of the veterans, another chap to have joined our club only in recent years.

The invitation from The Not Forgotten Association had been for three veterans and their partner/carer, which were allocated, but this chap kept on about how he'd like to attend and Di managed to secure a further invitation from the society, which had enough on its plate as it was with around two thousand guests to organise. The additional invitation was for a veteran only, without guest. I don't want to go into details, but Di was brought to tears by the abusive and completely uncalled for manner in which she was spoken to by a relative of this chap, who seemed to think that she had some God-given right to attend the event.

I feel a bit guilty about having pushed Di into the role. Gordon had not only been the club secretary, he had also organised several trips to Russia and was quite well known in Russian circles, having built up a lot of contacts. Di had reluctantly taken on the role of secretary to keep the club going, but she was never going to get involved in organising trips and the like. However, people kept telephoning her to request her help in either organising foreign visits or to make sure that their name was put down for future trips. She had one chap keep on at her that he wanted to go to Russia with twelve members of his family. She said that she was unable help him organise such a venture and he got quite shirty, saying that he had been told by somebody in Russia that she should help him.

Eugene, got in touch with me to say that he was organising a trip to St Petersburg in August 2014 for the unveiling of another monument to commemorate the convoys. He said that this would be a bronze statue of three sailors, a Russian, a Briton and an American[78] keeping watch together, and that the date of the ceremony was to coincide with the seventy-third anniversary of the arrival in Arkhangelsk of the first Arctic convoy.[79]

I said that I would like to go, but my sons, who had been supportive of everything I had done in recent years, were set against me making this trip. Each of them spoke to me to say that I was almost ninety and that I had been ill for many months after my previous trip – indeed, I have never properly recovered from the pneumonia I returned home with from Moscow. They pointed out the large sum of money that it had cost to get Tony home from the Moscow trip, and they asked how would I pay the bill should I be hospitalised and Eugene was unable to find a businessman to pick up the tab.

They said that they did not feel it would be fair on Di, and they were also concerned about the political situation, which, unfortunately, had taken a turn for the worse because of events in Crimea. They didn't want anybody possibly using me for their own political purposes.

It's hard for them to understand, but when you get to my age you want to take every opportunity that is offered to you – after all, who knows when it will be your last. Di said I should do whatever would make me happy, but I could see that she didn't really want me to go, and I decided that, perhaps, it would be better to stay at home. I think I would have managed the trip okay, but I understood why they were concerned. And, anyway, I can't complain. Look at what I had been able to do over the previous decade – how many people are fortunate enough to do even a fraction of that, let alone at my age?

Several of the chaps from our club went on the trip and enjoyed it. At least the weather was a lot better for them than it had been when we had gone to Moscow!

CHAPTER THIRTY

I marked my ninetieth birthday on 28th September, 2014. Some of my family organised a meal in a private section of a restaurant in Hampton, Middlesex, and thirty-two family members and friends came along to make it a nice evening.

Di's sister Joan and her daughter Tracey, had table place mats made from old photographs, including one of me as an air-gunner, and Steve printed off some pictures of me to which he attached some captions. He's quite good at that sort of thing – I have a picture of me with Tony Blair at Downing Street, with Blair allegedly saying to me, 'Apparently, all of Ten Downing Street's supply of whisky is missing... I've been told you probably know where it is'.

For my ninetieth, he poked a bit of fun at me with a few more pictures that were distributed among the guests. One showed Di holding our recently-born great-grandson, Jacob, with me sitting beside them. Di is looking intently at Jacob, and she is captioned as saying, 'Isn't he lovely?', to which my response was supposedly, 'Yes, I am'.

Unfortunately, I had a bit of bother eating my dinner because my wrist was in plaster as the result of a fall I'd had a few weeks previously. However hard we may try to fight it, time catches up with us all, and, since my return from Moscow in December, 2013 with pneumonia, I seemed to have suffered a variety of illnesses.

I tried to continue living the active life that I had always enjoyed, working on my garden and home, but after breaking my wrist I gradually became weaker. I was diagnosed with various chest complaints, which culminated in the discovery that I had two leaking heart valves. Since then, I have been in and out of hospital on several occasions, although the treatment I have received from Dr Sen (my GP), Dr Raffi Kaprielian (consultant cardiologist, West Middlesex hospital) and Professor Carlo Di Mario and his staff (Royal Brompton hospital) has been wonderful. They have helped to keep me going, and I can't thank them enough. If there was one good thing that came out of the war then it was the National Health Service. We must do everything we can to preserve this institution, something that makes me very proud to be British.

Life has been quite tough over the past year, and I find it particularly frustrating that I sometimes need to be pushed around in a wheelchair when I go out – anybody who knows me will tell you that isn't what I'm about. I have been married to Di for almost sixty years, and she never complains about all the things she has to do for me inside and outside the home, but I can see how it affects her.

My boys help out as much as they can, and I'm lucky to have them, along with our eight grandchildren and three great-grandchildren. I still see my sister Maureen and her husband Sylvester and their family, and I am very close to Joan and Derek, their children, grandchildren and great-grandchildren.

With the help of my family, I was able to play a small part in a couple of the commemorations in May 2015 to mark the seventieth anniversary of the end of the war in Europe. On Saturday 9th May, I took part in a moving service at the Russian

Memorial in the grounds of the Imperial War Museum, London. This was attended by a number of dignitaries and quite a few Russian people who live in London. They gave us flowers as a gesture of appreciation for the actions of the convoys, while the Russian Embassy presented each of us veterans in attendance with a medal to mark the anniversary. The following day, Sunday 10th May, I was very pleased to make it to St James' Park for the Royal British Legion's VE reception for two thousand veterans and guests. This event was superbly organised, and we were even given a commemorative picnic box! It was a lovely sunny day and Legion staff couldn't do enough for us. I was in my wheelchair, with Chris pushing and Di walking alongside us, when David Cameron came towards us in the opposite direction, surrounded by his bodyguards and officials. When he saw me, he stopped and knelt down to speak to me, saying something like, 'Thank you so much for all you did for all of us, it is so appreciated.' There was no media there, and I was glad about that because I think that showed it was genuine. Unfortunately, it all happened so quickly that Di and Chris didn't even get their cameras out.

I find it incredible that so many years have passed since the war was concluded and we were promised that a new peacetime life would begin for everyone! We all know what happened to that promise, and it saddens me to see so much trouble in the world – how quickly we seem to forget the lessons and sacrifices of the past.

I will never regret enlisting in the Fleet Air Arm and becoming an air-gunner, nor serving on the Arctic Convoys. I made so many good friends who shared those experiences with me – even if it took me a lot longer than it should have done to get back in touch after we went our separate ways in 1945. I am very proud that I played a part, however small, in helping the ordinary Russian people who suffered so much hardship and cruelty at the hands of others.[80]

I have never forgotten the years I spent serving my country, and I remember the good friends I made, and lost, in that time.

I have been lucky because I have lived a long and happy life, and can talk about my experiences to my family and anyone else who is interested in an old man's tale. One of the interesting projects I became involved in was for the charity Legasee,[81] which has compiled over one hundred video interviews of people who served in the war. I gave them a lengthy interview about my time in the Fleet Air Arm, and it appears on their website – so if you haven't had enough of me yet please take a look!

On my visits to Russia, I was privileged to visit several schools and colleges, where the students questioned me about my role during the war. This is something that I have also been honoured to do in England.

As I have said previously, I am not a great man of words, but I would like to say that I do take comfort from the fact that younger generations are still learning about the Second World War, and long may that continue. Only by remembering the sacrifices of the past can we hope to build a better future.

At some point in the not-too-distant future, all that will be left of those who served in the Second World War will be their memories. Nothing would give me greater satisfaction than those memories being used to help build a world that is safe and secure for my grandchildren, my great-grandchildren and the generations that will follow on from them.

TO RUSSIA...AND BACK

JAMES PITTS

REFERENCES

JAMES PITTS

1 Barnes is a suburban district in south-west London, to the north-east of the London Borough of Richmond upon Thames. It is 5.8 miles (9.3 km) south-west of Charing Cross in a loop of the River Thames. Barnes has a high proportion of eighteenth and nineteenth century properties, and, according to a survey in 2014, it has the highest proportion of independent shops of any area in Britain, at 96.6 per cent.

(Source: wikipedia.org)

Barnes is now one of the wealthiest districts in the UK. In August 2014, a two-bedroom cottage was for sale at the asking price of one million pounds, and a three-bedroom terraced house for one million, two hundred thousand pounds.

(Source: zoopla.co.uk)

2 Scarlet fever is an infectious disease caused by bacteria known as group A Streptococcus (GAS). GAS causes many infections, but the strain of GAS bacteria that causes scarlet fever is different because it produces a toxin that causes a red skin rash. Scarlet fever is more common in children (ages four to eight) than adults. The infection often starts in the throat and has the symptoms of a typical strep throat but goes on to produce the skin rash.

A proportion of people experience very severe disease that may include bacterial invasion into the bloodstream (sepsis), tissues, or bone. Severe disease was more common before the discovery of antibiotics and for centuries was a leading cause of death among children. Malnutrition, in either childhood or prenatally during pregnancy, was a risk factor for more severe disease. With the advent of the antibiotic era, mortality rates declined.

(Source: onhealth.com)

The mortality rate for scarlet fever for five to nine year olds in the 1920s was 6.6%.

(Source: hpa.org.uk)

3 Lillian Road, Barnes, was previously named Fanny Road but the road sign was stolen so many times that they felt it necessary to change the name.

(Source: theguardian.com)

4 Britain's economy in the 1920s struggled to pay for the huge cost of the First World War. In 1929, the US stock market crashed, causing world trade to slump, prices to fall and credit to dry up. The value of British exports halved and, by the end of 1930, unemployment had more than doubled to twenty per cent. Public spending was cut and taxes raised, but this depressed the economy and cost even more jobs. In 1931, the pound was devalued by twenty-five per cent.

(source: bl.uk)

5 Nitrous oxide, oxygen and ether were a popular sequence, and nitrous oxide and oxygen were often given to accompany local or regional blocks. Other uses of nitrous oxide as the sole agent were inevitably accompanied by hypoxaemia. The technique where induction was with one hundred per cent nitrous oxide and a small percentage of oxygen (usually less than ten per cent) added, was widely used for brief operations. The patient was invariably cyanosed and sometimes jacticated.

(source: bja.oxfordjournals.org)

6 Tuberculosis (TB) is an infectious disease transmitted through inhalation and is characterised by cough, fever, shortness of

breath, weight loss and the appearance of inflammatory substances and tubercles in the lungs. It is highly contagious and can spread to other parts of the body, especially in people with weakened immune systems. Incidence of the disease has declined since the introduction of antibiotics.

(Source: thefreedictionary.com)

At the beginning of the twentieth century, tuberculosis was one of the UK's most urgent health problems. TB was made a notifiable disease. There were campaigns to stop spitting in public places, and the infected poor were pressured to enter sanatoria that resembled prisons; the sanatoria for the middle and upper classes offered excellent care and constant medical attention. Whatever the purported benefits of the sanatoria, even under the best conditions, fifty per cent of those who entered were dead within five years.

(Source: wikipedia.org)

7 By 1930, there were five million radio sets in Britain but listeners had little alternative but to tune in to the BBC. Demand existed for popular music programmes, especially for dance band music and jazz, so the International Broadcasting Company (IBC) was set up to transmit popular programmes from Radios Lyon and Normandy, Radios Athlone, Méditerranée and Radio Luxembourg.

The Government and the BBC were hostile to these stations, but people tuned into them in increasing numbers. The Government pressured newspapers not to print their schedules, while the BBC was encouraged not to employ any artist or presenter who worked on a continental station.

The Government set up a committee in 1936 to look at all aspects of radio broadcasting, and it reported that, 'Foreign commercial broadcasting should be discouraged by every available means'. However, the overseas stations flourished and, by 1938, Radio Luxembourg had forty-five per cent of the Sunday listening audience against the BBC's thirty-five per cent, with advertisers spending £1.7m per annum, a substantial sum for those days.

(source: liverpoolmuseums.org.uk)

8 The early electricity supply industry in Britain was a patchwork of local electricity supplies provided by private companies and local authorities. The Electricity (Supply) Act 1926 increased central control of the industry by providing the legislation for the creation of a 'national gridiron', a 132kV high voltage transmission network. Managed by the Central Electricity Board (CEB), this evolved into the National Grid in 1938.

(Source: bl.uk)

9 Most of the modern domestic appliances in our homes today had been invented before 1945, but few people used them because they were expensive luxuries. Before the war, gas had become familiar to most people for cooking, water heating and lighting. Electricity take-up lagged behind gas until families moved into new houses with pre-wired electricity supplies. By 1938, the National Grid carried electricity across the country. War intervened, but eighty per cent of all households were connected by 1946. A supergrid in the 1950s brought electricity to nearly everyone.

(source: makingthemodernworld.org.uk)

10 The wide-ranging education act of 1921 raised the school leaving age to fourteen. The 1936 education act raised the leaving age to fifteen, although local education authorities were empowered to issue employment certificates to allow fourteen year olds

to work rather than attend school in certain circumstances, for example, where a family would suffer 'exceptional hardship' if the child did not work.

(Source: educationengland.org.uk)

11 The First World War started on 28th July, 1914. On 5th August 1914, Field Marshal Earl Kitchener of Khartoum took over as Minister for War. Six days later, 'Your King and Country need you: a call to arms' was published, calling for the first one hundred thousand men to enlist. The armistice with Germany was signed on 11th November 1918.

(Source: 1914-1918.net)

12 The Government introduced the Military Service Act in 1916, which specified enlistment for males aged nineteen to forty-one and had been unmarried or a widower on 2nd November, 1915. The act was extended to married men, and the lower age dropped to eighteen in May 1916.

(Source: 1914-1918.net)

13 The first official evacuations began on 1st September, 1939, two days before war was declared. A second evacuation was started in 1940 when, from 13th June to 18th June, around 100,000 children were evacuated (or re-evacuated). When the Blitz began on 7th September, 1940, children who had returned home or had not been evacuated were evacuated. London's population was reduced by nearly twenty-five per cent.

Evacuees were recommended to take the following items: Boys: two vests, two pairs of pants, Pair of trousers, two pairs of socks, six handkerchiefs, pullover or jersey. Girls: vest, pair of knickers, petticoat, two pairs of stockings, six handkerchiefs, slip, blouse, cardigan.

Also suggested for all children was: overcoat or mackintosh, comb, Wellington boots, towel, soap, facecloth, toothbrush, boots or shoes, plimsolls, sandwiches, packet of nuts and raisins, dry biscuits, barley sugar.

By the end of the war, more than three million people, mainly children, had experienced evacuation. Nobody was forced to go but parents were told that their children would be safer if they moved to the country.

(Source: woodlands-junior.kent.sch.uk)

14 Pre-war, each Sainsbury's store had six departments: dairy, bacon and hams, poultry and game, cooked meats, fresh meats and groceries.

There were two hundred and fifty-five shops at the outbreak of the Second World War, several of which were damaged by German bombs, prompting the creation of temporary stores.

(Source: encyclopedia.com)

15 Official rationing began on 8th January, 1940 with bacon, butter and sugar. Rations were distributed by weight, monetary value or points. One person's typical weekly allowance would be: one fresh egg, four ounces of margarine and bacon (about four rashers), two ounces of butter and tea; one ounce of cheese and eight ounces of sugar. Meat was allocated by price, so cheaper cuts became popular. Points could be pooled or saved to buy pulses, cereals, tinned goods, dried fruit, biscuits and jam.

(Source: bbc.co.uk/history)

16 Sperry in Britain started with a factory in Pimlico, London in 1913, manufacturing gyroscopic compasses for the Royal Navy, and becoming the Sperry Gyroscope Co Ltd in 1915. The company subsequently expanded to the Golden Mile, Brentford, in

1931, Stonehouse, Gloucestershire, in 1938 and Bracknell, Berkshire, in 1957. In 1963, these sites employed three thousand five hundred people. The Brentford site closed in 1967 and Stonehouse in 1969.

(Source: wikipedia.org)

17 The Home Guard was originally known as the Local Defence Volunteers (LDV). It was for men between seventeen and sixty-five years of age,and those young enough to be conscripted but who did not pass their military medicals could join. Men between seventeen and sixty-five years of age could join it. The Government had expected one hundred and fifty thousand volunteers in total but two hundred and fifty thousand applied to join in the first twenty-four hours.

By August, more than one million, five hundred thousand men had volunteered. To begin with, there were not enough official forms for men to apply, and police resorted to making a list of names. Because of a lack of weapons, the Home Guard was ordered to find whatever it could to defend itself. For a while, there was one rifle to every six men. When rifles did arrive, they were American P17s and P14s from World War One.

(Source: historylearningsite.co.uk)

18 Hounslow Heath once covered twenty-five square miles and was notorious for highwaymen, being peppered with gibbets. In 1919, the heath became the site of the first civil airport in the country. The earliest commercial flight was from Bristol to Hounslow and the inaugural scheduled air service was from Hounslow to Paris. The first flight to Australia left Hounslow in 1919, arriving twenty-eight days later. Commercial aviation moved to Croydon in 1920 and the airport closed. Hounslow Heath has long had a military connection.

(Source: hidden-london.com)

19 The German High Command launched 'the Blitz' on 7th September, 1940, in an attempt to demoralise the population and force Britain to come to terms. The intense bombing of London and other cities throughout the United Kingdom continued until 11th May, 1941. Residents sought shelter wherever they could find it, with many fleeing to the Underground stations that sheltered as many as 177,000 people during the night. In the worst single incident, 450 were killed when a bomb destroyed a school being used as an air raid shelter. The raids were only called off in order to move German bombers east in preparation for the invasion of Russia.

(source: eyewitnesstohistory.com)

From 7th October, 1940, to 6th June, 1941, a total of ninety high-explosive bombs landed on Brentford.

(Source: bombsight.org)

20 Telegraphist air-gunners (TAGS) started out in 1922 as part of the Royal Air Force's Fleet Air Arm. A TAG provided communication by Morse code and manned the rear gun. Three thousand TAGS were trained over twenty-eight years – four hundred and ninety-five were lost through enemy action and/or accidents and sixty-nine became prisoners of war. Most TAGS served only for the period of the Second World War and returned to their civilian occupations.

(Source: fleetairarmarchive.net)

21 The Royal Navy had was in the process of establishing its own aircrew training systems when war began in 1939. Aircrew candidates spent seven weeks at an induction centre, usually HMS St Vincent at Gosport, near Portsmouth, where they learned naval discipline, routines, customs, basic navigation, meteorology and signalling. Next was flying training.

Early in the war, all Fleet Air Arm basic flying training was handled by the Royal Air Force, but training also took place within the United States Navy's programme at Pensacola (even before the US entered the war), or within the British Commonwealth Air Training programme in Canada or Empire Air Training Scheme in New Zealand. Royal Navy aircrew trained in the US followed the same curriculum as their American counterparts.

Those trained in Britain, Canada or New Zealand spent eight weeks at elementary flying school. This was followed by ten to sixteen weeks of service flying training, using more advanced aircraft to study navigation, communications, gunnery, bombing, and night, instrument and formation flying. Graduates, who by then had accumulated about one hundred and fifty flying hours, received their commissions and returned to the Royal Navy's charge.

**(Source: Weapons and Warfare: Aircraft Carriers
by Paul E Fontenoy; abc-clio.com)**

22 Prior to the Second World War, what became the Royal Navy service camp at Astbury Park, New Jersey, had been holiday apartments for New Yorkers. The Royal Navy barracks comprised two hotels which were fenced and had a centre forecourt as a parade ground.

(Source: wartimeheritage.com)

23 The No.1 Naval Air Gunners School at Yarmouth, Nova Scotia, operated from January 1943 to March 1945. It was established at the request of the Admiralty to the Canadian authorities to see if a training school could be established to supplement the establishments in England that were training Royal Navy Telegraphist Air Gunners.

The administration was handled by the Royal Canadian Air

Force and the training by the Royal Navy. A branch of No.3 Operational Training Unit was located on the east side of the airport, meaning two establishments used the same airfield – East Camp for the training squadron, and West Camp, which was an operational Eastern Air Command station.

All training at the school ended on 19th March, 1945, and the station was officially closed on 30th March.

(Source: vintagewings.ca)

24 The Fairy Swordfish was a torpedo-carrying plane primarily carried on board British aircraft carriers. It was a bi-plane and, by the standards of the Second World War, it was slow and a veteran. However, it carried quite a punch.

Specifications: Crew: Three (pilot, observer, telegraphist air-gunner). Length: 36ft 4in. Wingspan: 45ft 6in. Height: 12ft 10in. Loaded weight: 9,2500 lb. Powerplant: 1 × Bristol Pegasus IIIM.3 radial engine, 690 hp (510 kW). Performance: Maximum speed: 139mph at 4,750ft. Range: 770 miles. Endurance: 5.7 hours. Service ceiling: 19,250ft. Climb to 5,000ft: 10 minutes. Armaments: either one 1,610-pound torpedo or one 1,500-pound mine or eight 110-pound bombs or six rocket projectiles; plus two .303 machine guns.

(Source: fleetairarm.com)

25 Prohibition was enacted across Canada from 1915 to 1917 under the War Measures Act. Once Prohibition laws were repealed, liquor sales and distribution were strictly controlled. People could drink at home, in private establishments such as labour clubs, private clubs and in hotel rooms but not public places. Liquor store windows were painted or heavily curtained.

During the Second World War, obtaining alcohol stocks was difficult, and beer parlours, private clubs and liquor stores often closed for several days at a time until the next shipment came in. When alcohol was available, long queues developed.

(Source: agingincanada.ca)

26 Morse code is named after Samuel F B Morse (1791-1872), who, along with Alfred Vail (1807-1859) and Joseph Henry (1797-1878), developed the electromagnetic telegraph and the code that assigns a set of dots and dashes or short and long pulses to each letter of the English alphabet.

The first working telegraph was produced in 1836. The first Morse Code message was sent from Washington to Baltimore in 1844.

It is used in emergencies to transmit distress signals when no other form of communication is available. The standard international distress signal is SOS – dot-dot-dot, dash-dash-dash, dot-dot-dot.

Experienced operators can easily converse at twenty to thirty words per minute.

(Source: omniglot.com)

27 In Canada, typically the lobster season peaks twice a year – once in the spring (April-June) and another in December. Each area is subject to its own season, which ranges from eight weeks to eight months. Canada accounts for more than 60 per cent of lobsters landings in North America and provides more than half of the world's supply of Lobster.

(Source: www.facebook.com/notes/lobster-tails/)

28 The Naval Auxiliary Air Facility Lewiston is located in Lewiston, Maine. It is a closed facility of the United States Navy. It was opened as a municipal airport but from late 1942 came under

the control of the US Navy. It was one of five air facilities to support Naval Air Station Brunswick, Maine, during the Second World War.

(Source: wikipedia.org)

29 Naval Air Station Squantum in Quincy, Boston, Massachusetts, was an active naval aviation facility in 1917 and from 1923-1953. The base was sited on Squantum Point and abutted Dorchester Bay, Quincy Bay, and the Neponset River. It was closed in 1953 when operations were moved to the nearby South Weymouth Naval Air Station.

Today, a marina sits on what was its northern end, while a 2,700-foot (820m) portion of the primary north-west runway was opened to the public in 2001 as Squantum Point Park. A local veterans' organisation maintains a small museum dedicated to preserving the memory of the station.

(Source: wikipedia.org)

30 The Fleet Air Arm 856 squadron was formed at Squantum, United States, in March 1944 as a torpedo bomber reconnaissance Avenger squadron, and subsequently embarked on HMS Smiter arriving at Machrihanish in June 1944. It was subsequently based at Maydown and Eglinton.

In September 1944, the squadron embarked on HMS Premier for operations off the Norwegian coast till March 1945. In April and May 1945 the squadron took part in Arctic Russia convoy duties on board HMS Premier, and after VE Day was intended for the 10th Carrier Air Group but was disbanded in June 1945.

(Source: fleetairarmarchive.net)

31 The Grumman TBF Avenger was an American-built plan that was also used by the Royal Navy's Fleet Air Arm. Though initially

known as the TBF Tarpon, the RN soon switched to the name Avenger. Beginning in 1943, British squadrons began seeing service in the Pacific as well as conducting anti-submarine warfare missions in the Atlantic and Arctic.

Specifications: Length: 40ft. 11.5in. Wingspan: 54ft. 2in. Height: 15ft. 5in. Empty Weight: 10,545 lbs. Loaded Weight: 17,893 lbs. Crew: 3. Performance: Power Plant: 1 × Wright R-2600-20 radial engine, 1,900 hp. Range: 1,000 miles. Max Speed: 275 mph. Ceiling: 30,100 ft. Armament: Guns: 2 × 0.50 in. wing-mounted M2 Browning machine guns, 1 × 0.50 in. dorsal-turret mounted M2 Browning machine gun, 1 × 0.30 in. ventral-mounted M1919 Browning machine gun. Bombs/ Torpedo: 2,000 lbs. of bombs or 1 Mark 13 torpedo.

(Source: militaryhistory.about.com)

32 HMS Smiter was a Ruler-class Escort Aircraft Carrier obtained under the US/UK Lend Lease/Lease agreement. The ship was laid down on 10th May, 1943 and launched on September 27 that year as USS Vermillion. She was fitted for service as an Escort Aircraft Carrier and formally handed over to the Royal Navy and commissioned as HMS Smiter. This name had not previously been use for a RN ship. US Navy radar outfits were fitted during build.

(Source: naval-history.net)

33 At the outbreak of the Second World War, the United States assumed a neutral stance. As Germany conquered much of Europe so the administration of President Franklin Roosevelt began seeking ways to aid Great Britain.

Initially constrained by the Neutrality Acts which limited arms sales to 'cash and carry' purchases, Roosevelt declared large amounts of US weapons and ammunition 'surplus' and authorised their shipment to Britain in mid-1940. Roosevelt was determined to provide Britain with all possible aid short of war, and he pushed for the creation of the Lend-Lease programme.

Officially titled An Act Further to Promote the Defense of the United States, the Lend-Lease Act was signed into law on 11th March, 1941. This allowed Roosevelt to authorise the transfer of military materials to Britain on the understanding that they would ultimately be paid for or returned if they were not destroyed.

In selling the program to the American public, Roosevelt compared it to loaning a hose to neighbour whose house was on fire. 'What do I do in such a crisis?' the president said. 'I don't say..."Neighbour, my garden hose cost me fifteen dollars; you have to pay me fifteen dollars for it". I don't want fifteen dollars — I want my garden hose back after the fire is over.'

Lend-lease was also offered to China for their war against the Japanese.

(Source: militaryhistory.about.com)

34 RAF Machrihanish was a Royal Air Force station located on the western side of the Kintyre peninsula to the west of Campbeltown. With the end of the First World War in 1918, the military left the area, and the aerodrome became a civilian operation, serving the growing number of private and pleasure flyers.

By the early 1930s, Midland & Scottish Air Ferries Ltd began to operate commercial flights from the airfield, which had become known under a variety of names, including Campbeltown Aerodrome. The outbreak of the Second World War saw the Royal Navy return to the area, requisitioning the original airfield and the area to its north.

A new airfield was built and named HMS Landrail. 772 Squadron (Fleet Requirement Unit), operating Swordfish torpedo bombers, was the first resident squadron to arrive there. Fleet Air Arm squadrons would disembark from their carriers, and proceed to HMS Landrail for training. The airfield made use of various firing and bombing ranges located around the coast of the Kintyre peninsula, such as the Skipness Bombing Range, used for practice runs, and the Balure Range, which was for live fire and bombing. The airfield also served as a base for convoy escort squadrons, and anti-submarine squadrons.

The end of the war saw the last squadron at HMS Landrail disbanded, and, by April 1946, the airfield had been reduced to care and maintenance, which meant it could be re-activated at any time.

(Source: secretscotland.org.uk)

35 The first V-1s were launched against London on 13th June, 1944. During the first V-1 bombing campaign, up to one hundred fell every hour on London. Over an eighty-day period, more than six thousand people were killed and seventeen thousand injured. One million buildings were wrecked or damaged. Unlike conventional aircraft bombing raids, V-1 attacks occurred around the clock in all types of weather, striking indiscriminately.

The 'V' came from the German word Vergeltungswaffen, meaning weapons of reprisal. They were nicknamed 'buzz bombs' due to the distinct buzzing sound made by their pulse-jet engines. Each V-1 was launched from a short length catapult then climbed to about three thousand feet at speeds up to three hundred and fifty miles per hour. As the V-1 approached its target, the buzzing noise could be heard on the ground.

At a pre-set distance, the engine would suddenly cut out and there would be momentary silence as the bomb plunged toward the ground, followed by an explosion of the 1,870-pound warhead. According to German records, more than eight thousand five hundred were launched against England, with about fifty-seven percent reaching their designated targets.

The remainder failed as a result of anti-aircraft guns, barrage balloons, and interception by fighter planes. Eventually, British and American planes knocked out the majority of the launching sites.

(Source: historyplace.com)

36 HMS Premier was a Ruler-class escort aircraft carrier obtained under the US/UK Lend-Lease/Lease Agreement. The ship was a C3 mercantile hull ordered by the US Navy and was converted during build for use as an Escort Aircraft Carrier. The ship was laid down on 31st October, 1942, and launched on 22nd March, 1943, as USS Estero.

She was renamed HMS Premier when formally transferred to the Royal Navy on 3rd November, 1943. She was fitted out for use as an Escort Carrier and fitted with US Navy radar outfits.

(Source: naval-history.net)

37 Scapa Flow is a natural harbour which has been used over many centuries and formed an important northern base for British fleets. During the Second World War, the Home Fleet was based at Scapa Flow, from where it helped to protect the Arctic Convoys to Murmansk.

In October 1939, HMS Royal Oak was attacked by U-boat in Scapa Bay. Torpedoes were fired, and a hole thirty feet in diameter was made in the hull. From the crew of one thousand four hundred men, eight hundred and thirty-three were killed. Following this, Scapa Flow became heavily fortified with anti-aircraft batteries, minefields and further blockships.

The Scapa Flow Visitor Centre is housed in the former oil pumping station at the Lyness Naval Base on Hoy. There are housed many exhibits from both World Wars.

(Source: scapaflow.co.uk)

38 German forces attacked Allied Arctic convoys until the very end of the war. Even though the country was being overrun in March and April 1945, U-boats continued to oppose convoys carrying supplies by sea to Murmansk in Russia. Northern Norway was the one place where the German navy had the forces to continue major operations.

(Source: cnrs-scrn.org)

39 For over three hundred years, the Royal Navy issued a daily 'tot' of Pusser's Rum to crews. It was first introduced into the Navy in 1655 as a substitute for beer, and by 1731 it was in general use. Pure rum was originally rationed out each day, but after 1740 it was watered down to two portions of water for every one of rum. The mixture became known as grog.

(Source: pussers.com)

40 In September 1944, Germany introduced the V-2 rocket, a liquid fuelled rocket that travelled at supersonic speeds and hurtled down toward its target at a speed of nearly four thousand miles per hour, smashing its two thousand-pound high explosive warhead into the ground without warning. V-2 rockets could not be intercepted. Over a thousand were fired at London.

(Source: historyplace.com)

41 On 16th April, 1945, Convoy JW-66, consisting of twenty-six merchant vessels, sailed for northern Russia. Its escort, commanded by Rear Admiral A B Cunninghame Graham, RN, comprised the cruiser HMS Bellona, the escort carriers HMS Vindex and HMS Premier, six destroyers, four corvettes, and a sloop. On 19th April, JW-66 was joined by three destroyers, four corvettes, and sixteen Russian submarine chasers from the Faroes. Initial contacts with the enemy proved spurious.

Throughout 22nd April, aircraft from HMS Premier and HMS Vindex flew around the convoy and at 19.55 a Swordfish aircraft was 'ditched' when its rocket-assisted take-off gear failed. The crew, however, was picked up by the escort. By 12.00 on 22nd April, JW-66 had reached 73° 27' N.18° 57' E. in the Bear Island Passage north of Norway.

On 24th April, the convoy steamed south-east towards Kola Inlet. From previous experience, as well as from decryption intelligence and radio traffic analysis, the Allies knew that there were a number of U-boats off the entrance to Kola Inlet and that JW-66 would most likely have to force its way into Murmansk.

The five ships of the 19th Escort Group had been sent ahead to meet the convoy off the entrance to Kola Inlet. At 11.30 on 25th April, after sweeping the approaches with sonar, the escorts met JW-66 and patrolled to the eastward until it had passed.

Screened by aircraft patrolling its flanks and dropping sonar buoys in front, JW-66 entered Murmansk while its escorts attacked sonar contacts and dropped depth charges at random. Twenty-six sonar contacts were attacked, including several mistaken assaults on fish, and more than 400 depth charges were expended by the British warships. Significantly, there were no attacks on Allied ships during the operation.

(Source: cnrs-scrn.org)

42 The daily rum ration continued through both world wars and beyond. However, with the increasing sophistication of military technology in the post-war period, the admiralty abolished the rum ration in 1970. The move was marked with sombre pageantry throughout the service on Friday, 31st July, which is often referred to as 'Black Friday' among sailors.

(Source: militaryhistorynow.com)

43 Murmansk is a seaport one hundred and twenty-five miles (200 km) north of the Arctic Circle, and on the eastern shore of Kola Bay, thirty miles (48 km) from the ice-free Barents Sea.

The town was founded in 1915 as a supply port in World War I, and was a base for the British, French, and American expeditionary forces against the Bolsheviks in 1918.

In the Second World War, Murmansk served as the main port for Anglo-American convoys carrying war supplies to the USSR through the Arctic.

It is now an important fishing port, and its fish-processing plant is one of the largest in Europe. Murmansk's ice-free harbour makes it Russia's only port with unrestricted access to the Atlantic and world sea routes. From December to May it replaces icebound St Petersburg as the major port of the northwest.

Murmansk is connected by railroad with St Petersburg and Moscow and the mining and industrial centres of Monchegorsk and Kirovsk. Major industries include fishing, fish processing, and shipbuilding.

Following the collapse of the Soviet Union in 1991, Murmansk's economy suffered, as major industries proved to be unprofitable under market economy conditions and most fishing vessels were contracted out to Norwegian and other foreign companies.

As a result, many people left the city, and in the 1990s the population dropped by more than one-fourth, though by the early 21st century the city had made a successful transition to a market economy.

Murmansk is the largest city in the world north of the Arctic Circle. Its population is around three hundred and twenty thousand.

(Source: britannica.com)

After Germany invaded the Soviet Union in 1941, Murmansk was just sixty miles east of the front line. This was the Soviet Arctic Fleet's main base and keenly desired by the Germans, who sent their elite XIX Mountain Corps under Generalmajor Eduard Dietl to advance over the rocky tundra, seize Murmansk and secure the northern front. However, the Allies' Arctic Fleet stymied Dietl with shore bombardments and amphibious landings behind German lines, bringing the German advances to a halt only halfway to their objective.

*(source: **The German Fleet at War, 1939-45** by Vincent O'Hara, Kindle edition)*

44 In 1945, the rationing system in Russia incorporated 80.6 million with workers' ration cards of the first and second class as well as special cards for civil servants, children and other dependants. The norms of distribution on ration cards and the prices of rationed products were strictly regulated. The daily norm of bread on a workers' card of the first class was 800 grams and of the second class 600 grams, while other norms were lower. Rye bread was a staple for most of the population.

(Source: Russia After the War: Hopes, Illusions and Disappointments, 1945-1957, by Elena Zubkova; University of Alabama)

45 On 26th April there were twelve U-boats off Kola awaiting the departure of the return convoy to Britain. The problem that confronted the Allies was how to get the return convoy past Kola Inlet.

Cunninghame Graham decided to try to trick the U-boats into thinking that the convoy was departing on the night of 27th/28thApril. The Russians turned on a number of lights and sent anti-submarine vessels into the inlet to drop depth charges, while the British warships sent dummy radio messages as if they were sailing. JW-66 finally sailed from Murmansk on the night of 29th April.

The ships of the 19th Escort Group were sent ahead to sweep Kola Inlet. The four escorts proceeded in line abreast formation, three thousand yards apart, searching for U-boats. HMS Loch Insh obtained a sonar contact at a range of 780 yards at 65°. The British frigate turned towards the target and attacked with a squid. U-307 surfaced and was attacked by HMS Loch Insh, Loch Shin, and Cygnet. It sank stem first.

HMS Goodall was torpedoed by U-968 with an acoustic homing torpedo that detonated its magazine. HMS Goodall did not sink immediately and HMS Honeysuckle and Farnham Castle rescued seventeen survivors. U-286 was then sunk.

RA-66, followed by the escort carriers HMS Premier and Vindex and the cruiser HMS Bellona, cleared Kola at 02.00 on 30th April.

There were a number of contacts with what were thought to be U-boats and a large number of attacks were carried out by the escorts.

On 1st May, German Air Force reconnaissance aircraft shadowed RA-66. On 2nd May, the U-boats were informed of the death of Hitler, and on 5th May, they were ordered to end operations against the Allies.

(Source: cnrs-scrn.org)

46 David Syrett, in his fascinating paper, *The Last Murmansk Convoys, 11 March-30 May 1945,* for The Northern Mariner, writes:

The last battles of World War II over Murmansk convoys were in some respects similar to the campaign waged by U-boats in British coastal waters during 1944-1945.

U- boats, equipped with schnorkels, once again hid in shallow water, thus avoiding detection by sonar and radar. But the battles off Kola were different from those in British waters because there were many more U-boats and ships involved. In the coastal campaign, single U-boats usually attacked individual Allied ships; in the battles off Murmansk wolf packs attacked Allied convoys.

Both sides benefited from communications intelligence. The Allies knew of U-boat deployment from decryption intelligence and radio traffic analysis, while the Germans, from their knowledge of Allied convoy cycles and radio traffic analysis, were aware of the approximate arrival times. Thus, the battles around Kola Inlet in the last weeks of World War II were not a surprise to either side. Nevertheless, in four arrivals and departures – JW-65/66 and RA-65/66 – the Germans only managed to destroy two merchantmen and two escorts.

This was an acceptable loss rate for the Allies and must be considered a failure for the Germans.

There were several reasons for this low casualty rate. Each encounter between the Allies and the U-boats lasted only a matter of hours – the time required for a convoy to depart or enter Kola Inlet – giving the U-boats only limited opportunities to attack. The Allies, knowing of U-boat deployments off Kola, used extremely strong escorts to force their way into and out of Murmansk. Further, even though the GAF (German Air Force) did shadow some convoys, German U-boats and aircraft proved incapable of pursuit or of mounting a sustained attack.

In the final analysis, the German navy could not prevent the Allies from shipping supplies to the Soviets through the port of Murmansk.

(Source: cnrs-scrn.org/northern_mariner)

47 Royal Naval Air Station Lee-on-Solent (HMS Daedalus) was one of the primary shore airfields of the Fleet Air Arm. It was first established as a seaplane base in 1917, and later became the

main training establishment and administrative centre of the Fleet Air Arm.

Situated near Lee-on-the-Solent in Hampshire, approximately four miles west of Portsmouth on the coast of the Solent, the establishment has since been closed.

(Source: forces-war-records.co.uk)

48 On 6th August, 1945, the United States used an atomic weapon against Hiroshima, Japan. This bomb, the equivalent of twenty thousand tons of TNT, destroyed ninety per cent of the city, killed an estimated eighty thousand people immediately and caused the death of tens of thousands more through radiation sickness.

On 9th August, 1945, another atomic bomb was dropped over Nagasaki, killing an estimated forty thousand people.

Emperor Hirohito announced Japan's unconditional surrender in a radio address on 15th August, citing the devastating power of 'a new and most cruel bomb.' 15th August, 1945 was, therefore, VJ Day.

(Source: history.com)

49 The Royal Hospital Haslar in Gosport provided medical care to service personnel of the Royal Navy, and later, to the Army, RAF, and civilians from 1753 until it was closed in 2009.

During the Second World War, the threat of air raids meant Haslar primarily treated emergencies who were then transferred to inland hospitals once the patient was out of immediate danger. In 1941, two bombs hit the hospital.

(Source: bbc.co.uk)

50 Barracuda attack aircraft were the first British aircraft of this

type to be constructed entirely of metal. They entered service on 10th January, 1943 and were found with British fleets in the Pacific Ocean and the Atlantic Ocean by 1944.

Although originally designed as torpedo bombers, they were more effective as dive bombers as the engine lacked the power to properly handle the weight of a torpedo during flight.

Later on in the war, a problem was discovered where leaking hydraulic fluid was producing ether fumes into the cockpits and disabling the pilots. After some fatal crashes, the decision was made to equip Barracuda aircraft with oxygen masks and require their use.

The last few remained in service with the Fleet Air Arm until mid-1950s.

(Source: ww2db.com)

51 On 6th February, 1958, twenty-three people, including eight players for Manchester United and three members of the club's staff died as a result of a plane crash at Munich airport.

Flying back from a European Cup tie against Red Star Belgrade, the team plane stopped in Germany to refuel. The first two attempts to take off were aborted, and, following a third attempt, the plane crashed.

Twenty-one people died instantly. Aeroplane captain Kenneth Rayment died a few weeks later, while footballer Duncan Edwards passed away 15 days after the crash.

Those from Manchester United who died were the players Roger Byrne (28), Eddie Colman (21), Mark Jones (24), David Pegg (22), Tommy Taylor (26), Geoff Bent (25), Liam Whelan (22) and Duncan Edwards (21), along with club secretary Walter Crickmer, trainer Tom Curry and coach Bert Whalley.

Eight journalists died: Alf Clarke, Tom Jackson, Don Davies, George Fellows, Archie Ledbrook, Eric Thompson, Henry Rose, and Frank Swift, who was a former Manchester City player. The plane captain, Ken Rayment, perished, as did Sir Matt's friend Willie Satinoff, travel agent Bela Miklos and crew member Tom Cable.

(Source: manutd.com)

52 Average UK house prices in 1958 were two thousand three hundred and ninety pounds.

(Source: thepeoplehistory.com)

53 A lumbar puncture is a medical procedure where a needle is inserted into the lower part of the spine to look for evidence of conditions affecting the brain, spinal cord or other parts of the nervous system.

(source: nhs.co.uk)

54 Viral meningitis can affect any age group but is more common in babies and children.

Many different viruses can cause meningitis, the most common of which live in the intestines and can commonly cause colds, sore throats, stomach upsets and diarrhoea. Only rarely do these viruses spread through the body to the meninges and cause meningitis.

Although most people make a full recovery, some are left with serious and debilitating after-effects that include headaches, exhaustion and memory loss.

The recovery process from viral meningitis can be very slow, although the majority of sufferers no longer experience after-effects within twelve months after their illness.

The symptoms of viral meningitis can be very similar to those of bacterial meningitis, so health officials say that it is essential to seek urgent medical help should anybody feels concerned.

(source: meningitisnow.org)

55 'The Troubles' refers to a thirty-year conflict in Northern Ireland that began with a civil rights march in Londonderry on 5th October, 1968, and concluded with the Good Friday Agreement on 10th April, 1998.

At its heart lay two mutually exclusive visions of national identity and national belonging.

During the Troubles, the scale of the killings perpetrated by all sides, including paramilitaries, exceeded three thousand six hundred. As many as fifty thousand people were physically maimed or injured, with countless others psychologically damaged.

(Source: bbc.co.uk)

56 Newport, Gwent, is approximately one hundred and twenty miles from Newport, Pembrokeshire.

(Source: maps.google.co.uk)

57 'In The Summertime' was the début single for Mungo Jerry. It was issued as a maxi-single, a seven-inch record played at 33.3RPM instead of the standard forty-five. Included on the disc were two other songs, 'Mighty Man' and 'Dust Pneumonia Blues'.

(Source: songfacts.com)

58 The British Home Championship (also known as the Home International Championship, the Home Internationals and the British Championship) was an annual football competition

contested between the United Kingdom's four national teams, England, Scotland, Wales and Northern Ireland (Ireland before its partition) from the 1883–84 season until the 1983–84 season. Northern Ireland competed as Ireland until 1976-77, when they officially changed their name. The 1980-81 Championship was cancelled due to civil unrest in Northern Ireland. Wins: England thirty-four (plus twenty shared), Scotland twenty-four (plus seventeen shared), Wales seven wins (plus five shared), Ireland/Northern Ireland three wins plus five shared).

(Source: myfootballfacts.com)

59 Decades later, I attended a sportsman's dinner in Northampton at which Roger de Courcey was a guest. I asked him to sign an autograph 'to the Gibson's gang' and gave it to Dad. Roger seemed surprised to be reminded of Bracklesham Bay, saying only, 'That was a long time ago!'

What was Gibson's is now South Downs Leisure Village, an adults-only holiday centre. On a visit to Bracklesham Bay in 2012, after a gap of nearly forty years, I was surprised at how recognisable the site was from my teenage years.

(Source: Steve Pitts)

60 The Britten-Norman BN-2 Islander is a 1960s light utility aircraft, regional airliner and cargo aircraft designed and originally manufactured by Britten-Norman. The Islander is one of the best-selling commercial aircraft types in Europe. They generally hold nine passengers and around seven hundred and fifty are still in service with commercial operators around the world.

(Source: Wikipedia.com)

61 Hounslow Football Club was originally named Hounslow Town, which had its own small stadium in Denbigh Road,

Hounslow, Greater London. The club was formed in 1946 and played in the Corinthian League, being league champions in 1949–50 and 1951–52. They were champions again in 1954–55, when they reached the first round of the FA Cup.

The club folded in 1991, and a school was built on the site. Hounslow merged with Feltham to form Feltham & Hounslow Borough, but the merged club reverted to the name Feltham in 1995. Feltham subsequently lost their home at the Glebelands, Feltham, and were amalgamated with landlords Bedfont Football and Social Club to become Bedfont & Feltham FC. Their home ground is The Orchards, East Bedfont.

(Source: Wikipedia.org)

62 The Fleet Air Arm memorial at Victoria Embankment Gardens, Whitehall, London is a bronze statue based upon Daedalus, who, in Greek mythology, crafted wings for himself and his son Icarus, only for the latter to fly so close to the sun that the wax melted and he fell into the sea. Kempster designed the memorial and Butler created the statue, which was unveiled by the Prince of Wales on 1st June, 2000.

On the memorial is inscribed: 'To the everlasting memory of all the men and women from the United Kingdom, the British Commonwealth and the many Allied Nations who have given their lives whilst serving in the Royal Naval Air Service and the Fleet Air Arm.'

(Source: londonremembers.com)

63 Awarded for service in World War Two, the Atlantic Star is a campaign medal of the British Commonwealth. The Star was to commemorate the Battle of the Atlantic which took place between 3rd September, 1939, and 8th May, 1945, while Allied convoys transporting goods and valuables from America and the colonies were under attack by German U-boats. The medal was

granted for 'six months' afloat in the Atlantic, Home Waters, parts of the South Atlantic and convoys to Russia.

Awarded to personnel of the Royal Navy and Merchant Navy, provided they had earned the 1939-45 Star for six months service in operational areas. The locations and areas differ from the Royal Navy and Merchant Navy to qualify for this campaign medal. Special conditions apply governing this award for those Naval personnel entering service less than six months before the end of the qualifying period, provided it was the last operational theatre that they would serve.

The Atlantic Star was also awarded to the RAF and aircrew who took part in operations against the enemy at sea within the qualifying areas, subject to two months service in an operational unit. However, the 1939-1945 Star medal must also be earned by the recipient before commencing qualifying service for the Atlantic Star medal.

(Source: forces-war-records.co.uk)

64 Commander Eddie Grenfell was the man who most veterans acknowledged and admired as the driving force behind the campaign for a separate medal for those who served on the Arctic Convoys.

He fought a long and ultimately successful campaign, and received his medal three months before he died at the age of 93 in June 2013. The Daily Mail newspaper marked his passing with the following story on 28th June, 2013:

'Commander Eddie Grenfell was the leading force in the 17-year fight to award a medal to 70,000 sailors whose service on what Churchill called 'the worst journey in the world' to Russia went unrecognised when the conflict ended.

His death came just three months after the survivors were finally presented with their Arctic Star medals by David Cameron. The retired naval officer passed away at his daughter

Trudie's home in Portsmouth yesterday. She said: 'I want to pay tribute to his determination, his tenacity and strength. He was a legend. He was an unstoppable force who fought for what he believed in and what was right.'

Cdr Grenfell, a radar operator, was serving on SS Empire Lawrence when she was torpedoed during one of the supply missions to ship arms to the Soviet Union in 1942. He was blown more than 30ft clear of the ship in the blast, then survived more than ten minutes in the freezing seas before he was rescued.

Trudie, 65, said her father had been in poor health and in and out of hospital for the past 18 months after he suffered a heart attack.

'He was a wonderful, wonderful gentleman with true spirit,' she added.

After the war, he was stationed at the British Embassy in Bonn, West Germany, and used his supreme naval knowledge to advise and rebuild the nation's navy along British lines.

The Peterhead-born sailor spent 35 years living in Germany, before returning to the UK in the late 1970s.

In the meantime, he had built up quite a following travelling Germany and giving lectures in schools about Henry VIII's Tudor warship, the Mary Rose, and his beloved adopted home of Portsmouth.

As an early volunteer for the Mary Rose Trust, Cdr Grenfell was instrumental in driving Portsmouth's burgeoning tourism industry and was lauded by civic leaders.

However, efforts to get him awarded an OBE never materialised.

In the mid-1990s, Cdr Grenfell was elected by fellow veterans to start a campaign for their own Arctic Star medal.

The war heroes, who faced a gauntlet of German U-boats and warplanes during the icy supply missions to Murmansk, were aggrieved that their efforts were lumped in with the separate Atlantic Campaign.

Some 3,000 sailors lost their lives in the vital missions, which were dubbed 'the worst journey in the world' by Winston Churchill.

Following the collapse of the Soviet Union, it was felt that time had come for an Arctic medal to be struck.

The campaign thrust Cdr Grenfell into the spotlight, and he attacked the mission with typical military vigour.

He often spent up to 18 hours a day writing letters to politicians, and inundated Downing Street with facts, figures and arguments outlining the veterans' injustice. His quest was strongly supported by his local newspaper The News in Portsmouth, which obtained a 46,000-signed petition and organised for 500 convoys survivors to march on Whitehall to call for a medal.

At one point, the octogenarian was given his own office in the paper's print room.

Despite numerous setbacks, the Labour government relented under public pressure and awarded an Arctic Star emblem badge in 2006.

However, the lapel badge was far from an official medal and Cdr Grenfell fought on.

His campaign received renewed vigour in 2010 when the Coalition Government came to power.

Previous Conservative leaders Michael Howard and Iain Duncan Smith had backed the cause, and made public promises that a Tory government would finally strike a medal.

However, now aged 91 years, Cdr Grenfell still had to fight for another two and a half years before the campaign was finally won.

During that time, he clashed publicly with the armed forces

minister Andrew Robathan and accused David Cameron of betraying the Tory party's medal promise.

It was typical of the man, whose soft Scottish voice belied the fire which burned ferociously in his belly.

Finally, after an independent Whitehall review, Mr Cameron announced last December that a new Arctic Star would be struck.

Cdr Grenfell was by this time in rude health following his heart attack and could not travel to Downing Street to be given his medal.

Civic leaders instead honoured him with a special event held at Portsmouth Guildhall earlier this year, which was the last time Cdr Grenfell was seen in public.

The Chief of Defence Staff General Sir David Richards paid tribute to Cdr Grenfell yesterday.

The UK's most senior military officer presented Cdr Grenfell with his Arctic Star at a ceremony at Portsmouth Guildhall in March this year.

General Sir David Richards said: 'I was delighted and truly humbled to be able to present Commander Eddie Grenfell with his Arctic medal in Portsmouth in March.

'Eddie was a young sailor when he endured the hardships of the Arctic convoys which Winston Churchill called the worst journey in the world.

'It is in great part through his tireless efforts that the achievements and endurance of those involved in the convoys have been recognised.'

The Second Sea Lord Vice-Admiral David Steel said: 'I was greatly saddened to hear Cdr Eddie Grenfell has passed away.

'He fought bravely for our country in the Second World War, especially on the Arctic Convoys, and he fought just as valiantly to gain the recognition for his comrades, who endured the terrible hardships of those convoys, that they so richly deserved.

'I am thankful that he was able to receive his Arctic Star from the Chief of Defence Staff back in March before his passing.

'On behalf of the Royal Navy, I would wish to pass my sincere condolences to his family.'

(Source: dailymail.co.uk)

65 The Arctic Emblem was commissioned to commemorate the service of Merchant Seamen and members of the Armed Forces in the icy waters of the Arctic Region between 3rd September, 1939, and 8th May, 1945. At the time of its announcement, the Ministry of Defence said: 'Service in the Arctic during the Second World War was recognised by the award of campaign stars at the end of the war. Those who served in the campaign in Norway in 1940 qualified for the 1939-45 Star on entry into theatre (instead of having to complete six months' operational service as was usual for that Star). In addition, the criteria for the Atlantic Star specifically included service on the convoys to North Russia. There are no plans to introduce any new medals for Second World War service.'

(Source: veterans-uk.info)

66 There was a strong reaction to the decision to award an emblem rather than a medal.

On 8th March, 2005, The Telegraph printed the following story:

'Veterans of the Arctic Convoys, some of the most dangerous operations undertaken by British seamen during the Second World War, are to be honoured by a simple badge rather than the medal they have been fighting for.

The decision, announced last night by Tony Blair, was greeted with dismay by many of the 200 campaign survivors who attended a reception at No 10 marking the 60th anniversary of its conclusion. Some said the badge was a pre-election stunt.

Eddie Grenfell, a former commander in the Royal Navy who as a young seaman narrowly avoided freezing to death after his ship was sunk in the Arctic, is leading the fight to have the convoys recognised as separate from the Battle of the Atlantic.

He said: 'Nothing but a medal will do. The Russian convoys were a distinct episode in the war and form the only campaign not to be commemorated by a separate medal. It is amazing that British seaman involved have received their only honour from Russia, which has issued anniversary medals.

'If Mr Blair thinks we will be happy with a glass of sherry he had better think again. We have no intention of giving up.'

More than 20,000 Royal Navy and Merchant Navy personnel participated in the almost 80 convoys that took armaments and other supplies to the Soviet Union between 1941 and 1945. Some 3,000 men perished in the Barents Sea, where survival was measured in minutes.

Despite their sacrifices and the support of 428 MPs, the 3,000 British survivors of the campaign have failed to persuade the Ministry of Defence of their case.

The MoD, which relies on a decision in the 1940s to include the Arctic in the area covered by the Atlantic Star, was unrepentant.

A spokesman said: 'We do not feel it is appropriate to issue a separate medal.'

(source: telegraph.co.uk)

67 Victory Day in Russia is celebrated on 9th May and is the country's second most popular public holiday after New Year's Day.

The holiday marks the capitulation of Nazi Germany to the Soviet Union in the Second World War, known in Russia as the

Great Patriotic War, in 1945. Unlike most of Europe, where it is celebrated on 8th May, Victory Day in Russia is celebrated on 9th May as Germany's surrender was signed late in the evening on 8th May, 1945, when it was already 9th May in Russia.

It was first celebrated in fifteen Soviet republics but only became a non-labour day in 1965.

It commemorates the millions of people who lost their lives and honours the bravery of the Russian people – it is often said that there was not a single family in the country who did not lose someone in that war.

(Source: rbth.co.uk)

68 The Medal of Ushakov is a state decoration of the Russian Federation that was retained from the awards system of the USSR post 1991. It is awarded to soldiers and sailors of the Navy and of the Border Guard Service of the Federal Security Service of the Russian Federation for bravery and courage displayed while defending the Motherland and the public interests of the Russian Federation in naval theatres of military operations, while protecting the state borders of the Russian Federation, in carrying out naval combat missions with vessels of the Navy and/or Border Guard Service of the Federal Security Service of the Russian Federation, during exercises and manoeuvres in the performance of military duties under conditions involving a risk to life, as well as for excellent performance in naval combat training.

The British government initially refused permission for British personnel to receive the medal because it said the honour went against rules governing medals given by other countries, but in 2013 the awarding of the Ushakov medal was made an exception to these rules.

(Source: rusemb.org.uk)

69 The Not Forgotten Association is a national tri-service charity which provides entertainment, leisure and recreation for the serving wounded, injured or sick and for ex-service men and women who have been affected by conflict or by subsequent injury.

It runs a wide and varied programme of activities including outings, concerts, holidays, events and the provision of televisions and TV licences, and each year helps and supports approximately 10,000 individuals of all ages.

(Source: nfassociation.com)

70 The Mariinskiy Palace was commissioned in 1839 by Emperor Nicholas I as a wedding gift for his daughter, Grand Duchess Maria Nikolaevna, who married Duke Maximilian of Leuchtenberg, the step-grandson of Napoleon Bonaparte.

It occupies a prominent position in St Petersburg's historic centre, across St Isaac's Square and the Blue Bridge from St Isaac's Cathedral.

Court architect Andrey Stackensneider, who was responsible for the Nikolaevskiy Palace and the Beloselskiy-Belozerskiy Palace, created a neoclassical building with intricate décor inspired by medieval French and Renaissance architecture.

The palace has been used as a government building since March 1917, originally as home to the Council of the Russian Republic under the Provisional Government. During the Second World it was used as a hospital and was badly bombed. It then became the residence of the Leningrad Soviet, and has housed the St Petersburg's Legislative Assembly since 1994.

(Source: Saint-petersburg.com)

71 Andrew Robathan was subjected to intense criticism after his performance in the House of Commons on 6th December,

2011, in which he responded to a request for the Arctic Star campaign medal by saying: 'We have taken the view in this country, traditionally, that medals will only be awarded for campaigns that show risk and rigour.'

Among the many Daily Mail articles and comments which followed, the following appeared on 11th December 2011:

'Defence Minister Andrew Robathan should be sacked over his insult to the heroes of the Arctic Convoys, veterans said last night.

He sparked anger by comparing the Second World War veterans' claim for a medal to the large number of honours 'thrown around' by Libyan dictator Colonel Gaddafi and Iraqi tyrant Saddam Hussein.

The beleaguered minister made the disparaging remarks after Tory MP Caroline Dinenage urged the Government to keep its pre-election pledge to honour the sacrifice by striking a specific Arctic Medal.

Yesterday even his boss, Defence Secretary Philip Hammond, distanced himself from the comments.

He told the Commons' defence select committee: 'I don't think he intended to cause any offence but there was an unfortunate juxtaposition of words. The role of the Arctic convoys is well known and if any offence has been caused I deeply regret that.'

More than 3,000 British sailors died on the convoys to keep the Soviet Union supplied and fighting on the Eastern Front. They braved treacherous freezing seas and ran a deadly gauntlet of Nazi U-boats and warplanes.

Of 1,400 ships on 78 convoys – described by Winston Churchill as 'the worst journey in the world' – 101 perished in the icy waters north of Norway.

Veterans Minister Mr Robathan, a former soldier who was awarded a medal for running a prisoner-of-war camp in the first

Gulf War, faced a clamour of demands for his resignation after likening the Arctic medal campaign to notorious authoritarian regimes which handed out so many medals it diminished their worth.

He said: 'Medals in the UK mean something. Authoritarian regimes and dictators often throw around a lot of medals.

'One can look, for instance, at North Korean generals who are covered in medal ribbon, or Gaddafi, or Saddam Hussein. We have taken the view in this country, traditionally, that medals will only be awarded for campaigns that show risk and rigour. Some regimes give out very large numbers of medals whereas we, traditionally, do not.

But Commander Eddie Grenfell, 91, the leader of the Arctic Medal campaign, said: 'He cannot get away with the fact he said those dreadful things about the Arctic veterans. The man should be sacked from his job.

'He has failed in his duty. He is not the veterans minister; he is the minister against veterans.'

Falklands veteran Simon Weston said: 'The minister should think long and hard about resigning over this terrible insult. It was a cheap shot.

'The men on the convoys selflessly went into some of the most harrowing conditions with the knowledge that they could be hunted down and blown up by German U-boats. To suggest they are in any way like Gaddafi's henchmen is indefensible.'

Gemma Doyle, a Labour defence spokesman, said: 'These are sick comments and a slap in the face to the heroes who took part in one of the most perilous campaigns in the Second World War.

'For anyone to insult them is unacceptable, but for the veterans minister to do so is outrageous.'

Lieutenant Commander Dick Dykes, 92, who took part in the Arctic Convoys aboard HMS Honeysuckle, said: 'It was a disgusting thing to say. He doesn't deserve to be in the job.'

Miss Dinenage, who has backed the convoy veterans' medal battle for a decade, said: 'The words were extremely ill-judged. It is impossible to overstate the sacrifices that these men made and the hardships they endured to secure the freedoms we take for granted.

Some 66,500 men took part in the convoys. If they had failed to deliver the supplies and equipment, Hitler could have defeated the Red Army and turned his full military might against Britain. Only around 200 veterans are still alive, all in their 80s and 90s.

Successive governments have rejected pleas for an Arctic medal claiming the sailors had already been recognised for the separate campaign in the Atlantic.

After being criticised, Mr Robathan tried to defuse the row but stopped short of apologising.

He said: 'There was no intention to cause any offence. I was making the point that we honour people for their service in a very different way to that of authoritarian regimes.

A Ministry of Defence spokesman said: 'The Government has committed to a fresh review of the rules governing the award of military medals. This review will be conducted by an independent reviewer with full consultation with interested parties.'

(Source: dailymail.co.uk)

72 Caroline Dinenage is the Conservative Member of Parliament for the constituency of Gosport, Stubbington, Lee-on-the-Solent, and Hill Head. After contesting the Portsmouth South seat in 2005, she was selected in one of only two all-postal ballot Open Primaries to be the Conservative candidate for Gosport. She was elected in May 2010 with a majority of 14,413 votes and returned to the House of Commons in May 2015 with an increased majority of 17,098.

(Source: conservatives.com)

73 Victory Day London was conceived on 1st May 2007 with the sole idea to mark the 9th May in London as it is traditionally celebrated in Russia. Starting 9th May 2008, the event focused on the Arctic Convoys with the aim to promote and propagate the legacies of the achievements of and everyone involved.

(Source: victorydaylondon.co.uk)

74 The Museum of the Great Patriotic War is located in the Park of Victory on Moscow's Poklonnaya Gora. It commemorates both the suffering and losses of the Soviet Union and the heroism of soldiers of the Red Army between the years 1941 and 1945.

A competition for the design of a memorial complex in honour of the expected victory was announced during the war, but it wasn't until 1961 that the Park of Victory was laid out on the Poklonnaya Gora. The park was originally dedicated to the 1812 victory over Napoleon, but an additional dedication was instated in March 1986, when the Soviet Ministry of Culture decided on the establishment of the Central Museum of the Great Patriotic War.

The museum was opened on 9th May, 1995, on the fiftieth anniversary of the end of the war. Fifty-five heads of state attended the opening, including US president Bill Clinton. The museum contains a Hall of Names with memorial books listing the names of over twenty-six million dead from the Soviet Union, a memorial hall for soldiers and the twelve 'hero cities' of the Soviet Union.

(Source: memorialmuseums.org)

75 The Olympic torch went on a journey of one hundred and twenty-three days and sixty-five thousand kilometre from Olympia, Greece, starting on 2nd October 2013. It arrived at its final destination, Sochi, on 7th February, 2014, the eve of the

opening ceremony for the XXII Olympic Winter Games.

Fourteen thousand torch-bearers carried the flame, which travelled over land, sea and air, and took in all eighty-three regions of the Russian Federation.

(source: olympic.org)

A total of one hundred and thirty torch-bearers carried the Olympic flame through the streets of Severodvinsk and Arkhangelsk on 1st November 2014. Thousands of people turned out to watch the torch-bearers carry the flame along a route that included the historic streets of the Pomorye capital before a public celebration at the city's Sports Palace.

(source: dvinanews.ru)

76 HMS Belfast was originally commissioned into the Royal Navy as a light cruiser on 5th August, 1939.

From that time until the ship was opened to the public in 1971, the vessel had many and varied roles from protecting Arctic Convoys in the Second World War, to evacuating survivors of Japanese prisoner of war camps and serving in the Korean War.

HMS Belfast was ordered in 1936 by the Admiralty along with her sister ship HMS Edinburgh. They were 'Southampton' class large light cruisers, with six-inch guns and a displacement of ten thousand tons. The ship was constructed by shipbuilders Harland and Wolff of Belfast and launched by Anne Chamberlain, the Prime Minister's wife, on 17th March 1938.

In August 1939, after fitting out and builder's trials, HMS Belfast was finally commissioned into the Royal Navy. The cost was £2,141,514 for the build, including £75,000 for the guns and £66,500 for aircraft.

In September 1939, HMS Belfast was sent to Scapa Flow as part of the 18th Cruiser Squadron. She patrolled the Northern

Waters and captured the German liner SS Cap Norte which had been disguised as the Swedish ship Ancona (a neutral vessel).

HMS Belfast's initial period of active service came to a sudden end on 21st November, 1939 when she was hit by the detonation of a magnetic mine. It took three years to repair her ready for action.

Once repaired, Belfast had been turned into the largest and most powerful cruiser in the Royal Navy – her displacement was increased to 11,500 tons, and she was given the most up-to-date radar and fire control systems. She joined the 10th Squadron for most of 1943, in the icy waters of the Arctic, and was tasked with providing protection for Arctic convoys to the Soviet Union.

HMS Belfast is famous for her part in the sinking of the German battle cruiser Scharnhorst on 26th December, 1943. Thanks to British intelligence, the navy knew that the Scharnhorst was planning to attack our convoys. The command were able to put British war ships and cruisers (including HMS Belfast) in place so that the German ship was cut off, and eventually HMS Belfast and HMS Jamaica were given the order to sink her with torpedoes.

The raid on the German battleship Turpitz in northern Norway in March 1944 is also one of HMS Belfast's successful missions. She was part of the powerful force which destroyed Germany's last surviving heavy battleship.

HMS Belfast played her part in the D-Day landings in Normandy on 6th June 1944. For five weeks she supported the ships involved in this assault, and she is said to have fired one of the first shots on D-Day.

During the Korean War, HMS Belfast spent over four hundred days on active patrol supporting the retreating American and South Korean troops.

After this, she had a major refit in Devonport Dockyard to

prepare her for peace-keeping duties.

In 1963, she was retired and reclassified as a harbour accommodation ship. HMS Belfast was saved from the scrap-yard by an independent trust headed up by one of her former captains, Rear-Admiral Sir Morgan Morgan-Giles. This trust campaigned for many years to save the ship until she was finally brought to London and opened to the public on 21st October 1971. In 1978, HMS Belfast became a branch of the Imperial War Museum.

(Source: aboutbritain.com)

77 The North Caucasus is the northern part of the Caucasus region between the Black Sea and the Caspian Sea and within European Russia. The term is also used as a synonym for the North Caucasus economic region of Russia.

(Source: www.britannica.com)

78 Although the Arctic Convoys were run between Britain and Russia, the United States was heavily involved in supplying the Soviet Union with essential equipment. The convoys carried a total of fifteen thousand aircraft, seven thousand tanks, three hundred and fifty tons of explosives and fifteen million pairs of boots supplied by the United States.

(source: usmm.org/ww2)

79 The Royal Navy's presence in the Arctic was first made known in August 1941 when submarines started operating with some success against German shipping supporting the Axis attack from Norway towards Murmansk. The first convoy sailed in that month and several more followed that year, with the loss of only one ship. However, the picture changed considerably the following year as the U-boats launched repeated raids on the

convoys. In total, eighty-five merchant vessels and sixteen Navy warships were lost and some three thousand British sailors perished.

(source: naval-history.net)

80 The web pages of the Embassy of the Russian Federation to the United Kingdom of Great Britain and Northern Ireland has a section dedicated to the Arctic Convoys. To help explain the extent to which the convoys are valued by the Russians, I have extracted a few paragraphs from the web page entitled 'Arctic Allied Convoys'. These are below:

For the gruelling years of the Second World War the Soviet, British, American, Canadian, South African and other military and merchant sailors ploughing the Arctic seas within the Convoys discharged their allied duty with honour.

A convoy set off each month, except in the summer when the lack of darkness made them very vulnerable to attack. On the other hand, in the darkness of the Arctic winter, when the sun never rose, keeping station was difficult for the poorly equipped merchant ships, so there was always a danger of ship-to-ship collision.

Sailing around the northern tip of Norway, the convoys would be exposed to one of the largest concentrations of German U-boats, surface raiders and aircraft anywhere in the world. Strict orders forbade the halting of any ship for even a moment for fear of being attacked by prowling German U-boats, and individuals who fell overboard or survivors seen adrift on the waters had to be ruthlessly ignored. Each delivery of arms was an epic achievement, described as undertaking the impossible.

The Allied seamen showed true heroism in their long and perilous sea passages in convoys, being constantly attacked by enemy forces in the appalling weather conditions of the Arctic. The bravery of these men and women who unsparingly fought for the Victory will be always remembered and respected.

(source: rusem.org.uk/artcticalliedconvoys)

81 Legasee is an independent charity funded through private donations and the creation of innovative educational projects. Its commitment is that future generations can learn about British military history through the personal recollections of the men and women who witnessed it first hand. Legasee's constitution is 'to advance the education of the public in the subject and effects of military activity and to promote the conservation of records of veterans personal experiences and comment for future benefit'.

(source: www.legasee.org.uk)